The
Nimble Collaboration

Fine-Tuning Your Collaboration for Lasting Success

The Nimble Collaboration

Fine-Tuning Your Collaboration for Lasting Success

by Karen Ray

AMHERST H.
WILDER
FOUNDATION

SAINT PAUL,
MINNESOTA

Published with the support of The David and Lucile Packard Foundation
and the Amherst H. Wilder Foundation.

The Amherst H. Wilder Foundation is one of the largest and oldest endowed human service and community development organizations in America. For more than ninety years, the Wilder Foundation has been providing health and human services that help children and families grow strong, the elderly age with dignity, and the community grow in its ability to meet its own needs.

We hope you find this book helpful! Should you need additional information about our services, please contact: Wilder Center for Communities, Amherst H. Wilder Foundation, 919 Lafond Avenue, Saint Paul, MN 55104, phone (651) 642-4022.

For information about other Wilder Foundation publications, please see the back of this book or contact:

Publishing Center
Amherst H. Wilder Foundation
919 Lafond Avenue
Saint Paul, MN 55104

1-800-274-6024
www.wilder.org

Edited by Vincent Hyman and Doug Toft
Designed by Kirsten Nielsen
Cover design by Rebecca Andrews

Manufactured in the United States of America

First printing, July 2002

Library of Congress Cataloging in Publication Data

Ray, Karen Louise, 1952-
 The nimble collaboration : fine tuning your collaboration for lasting success / by Karen Ray.
     p. cm.
Includes bibliographical references.
  ISBN 0 940069 28 8 (pbk.)
  1. Joint ventures. 2. Partnership. 3. Interorganizational relations. I. Title.
  HD62.47 .R39 2002
  658'.044—dc   212002004494

About the Author

KAREN RAY is president of Karen Ray Associates, a consulting firm that specializes in training and organization development for government, community, and nonprofit agencies. She holds a master's degree in applied behavioral sciences from Whitworth College, Spokane, Washington, with a specialty in organization and human development.

From 1977 to 1983 Karen was executive director of a literacy-focused agency mandated to collaborate by state and federal funders. Her consulting practice began when she decided to combine this collaborative experience with her training expertise to problem-solve with agencies involved in joint ventures. Collaboration is now the theme of her work with organizations in many states. Karen trains others in collaboration workshops and provides consulting services to ongoing collaborations.

Based on research conducted by the Wilder Foundation and on personal experience, Karen coauthored *Collaboration Handbook: Creating, Sustaining, and Enjoying the Journey* with Michael Winer in 1994. This award-winning book guides nonprofit staff through partnership ventures.

Karen Ray may be contacted at thenimblecollab@visi.com.

Acknowledgments

This book would not have been possible without contributions from editors Vince Hyman and Douglas Toft. Many thanks to all the staff of the Wilder Publishing Center for their work in producing a pleasing, easy-to-read manual.

A special thanks to those people who reviewed the field-test draft of this book:

Emil Angelica	Curt Milburn
Brian Cole	Anita Miller
Joseph Connor	Jessica Parker-Carlson
Pam Curtis	Bill Potapchuk
Gary Ellis	Mary Sabatke
Mary Heiserman	Julie Suchy
Louis Hohlfeld	Patty Wilder
Stephanie Kadel-Taras	L'Tanya Williamson
Amelia Kohm	Michael Winer
Cathy Lindsley	

This book is dedicated to the professionals who work hard to collaborate in many different arenas. Their stories and the work we did together inspired *The Nimble Collaboration*.

Contents

About the Author v

Acknowledgments vii

Introduction: Collaborations Can Be Nimble 1

New Expectations Drive Collaboration 1

Four Stages in Starting a Collaboration 3

Enter the Nimble Collaboration 4

Nimble Collaboration Renews Institutions 5

Use Three Strategies to Become Nimble 6

Apply These Strategies to Two Types of Collaboration 7

Get the Most From This Book 10

**PART I   To Become Nimble, Focus on Results,
Relationships, and Resilience** 13

Chapter One: Focus on Results 15

Consider Your Premise 15

Consider Your Promise 18

State Your Mission 20

State Your Vision 22

State Your Desired Results as Outcomes 23

State Your Evaluation Criteria 23

Create Your Work Plan 25

Chapter Summary 32

Chapter Two: Shape Relationships 33

Build Trust 33

Reveal Your Self-Interest 34

Invite All Orgainzations That Can Contribute 38

Define Core Organizations 39

Clarify Roles 41

Plan to Communicate Key Information 51

Chapter Summary 52

Chapter Three: Structure for Resilience **55**

Consider Ten Principles of Resilience 56

Refine Your Process for Making Decisions 58

Share Financial Information 64

Create a Nimble Governance System 69

Chapter Summary 74

Actions for the Nimble Collaboration **76**

**PART II Applying Nimble Strategies to
Real-Life Collaborations** **79**

Chapter Four: Collaborate to Integrate Services **81**

Know When You're Really Working
on Service Integration 84

Recognize Three Points of Service Integration 85

Chapter Summary 96

Chapter Five: Collaborate to Resolve Complex Issues **97**

Use These Emerging Best Practices 98

Chapter Summary 106

Conclusion: The Power of Collaboration **107**

Appendix A: Sample Forms **109**

Program Financial Information 111

Write a Memo of Agreement for Your Collaboration 113

Draft a Formal Governance Agreement 115

Appendix B: Resources **119**

Introduction

Collaborations Can Be Nimble

This book emerged from the experiences of people like you—people who take part in collaborations that are fraught with frustrations and rich with celebrations. For almost twenty years, I've been listening to collaboration partners ask themselves questions: *"What do successful collaborations do? Can partnerships be clever, agile, and responsive? Can we find effective ways to manage our work together and act quickly when we need to?"* As my colleagues and I found answers to these questions, we discovered that "capable collaboration" is not an oxymoron. The result is this book about constructing a particular kind of collaboration, one that is satisfying and productive. One that leads to systems change and engages its member organizations in reinventing themselves for the good of their customers and of their staff.

One adjective describes such remarkable collaborations: *nimble*. The *American Heritage Dictionary* defines nimble as "Quick in movement or action . . . deft." The word *nimble* also implies cleverness in understanding, being flexible, and being responsive. I apply nimble to collaborations as follows:

> The nimble collaboration is based on *results* that are clearly defined, *relationships* that are deft, and a structure that is *resilient*, leading to productive action.

Every sentence in this book is here for one reason—to help you "nimble-ize" your collaboration as quickly and efficiently as possible by focusing on "the three Rs" of nimble collaborations: results, relationships, and resiliency.

New Expectations Drive Collaboration

If you were part of an active collaboration ten years ago, you were an unusual person with unusual support from your boss or board. Ten years ago, collaborations were hard to start and even harder to keep up. They made individuals and organizations share information and work together in unusual ways.

Today, working in collaboration is considered a must for many organizations. Museums and galleries are working with government units to promote arts. Public health departments are providing services for children on elementary school campuses. Social services agencies are establishing offices in libraries. And foundations are investing in collaborations in order to push systems to change faster and wiser. Collaborations of different sizes and purposes exist in countless communities across the nation.

The reasons for collaboration are to achieve some result your organization cannot achieve alone, and to achieve that result in a complex environment. You can collaborate to

- Respond to the requirements of a funder or a legal mandate that instructs you to "work collaboratively."
- Save money on back-office functions—for example, rent, technology, and support services such as accounting.
- Better serve clients. Many collaborations are motivated by a desire to provide a more responsive set of products, or more culturally competent services, or to fulfill a neglected area of need.
- Respond to a crisis, such as a flood, an act of terrorism, or a sudden acceleration of drug use among teens.
- Improve a system. Unified case management, one-stop shopping for social services, and wrap-around services are all code phrases for improving a system's ability to work more quickly, more creatively, or more cost-effectively.
- Improve a community. Housing developers and cities redesign urban spaces, manufacturers and ecologists focus on clean water tables for several states at once, churches and schools promote cross-cultural respect.

Still, for many of us, the collaboration process is a pain in the neck. Collaboration can mean frequent, irritating meetings, arduous task completion, and snail-paced decisions. These challenges can slay collaborations that don't pay attention to the new environment for collaboration.

Times have changed, and the barriers to collaborations that existed ten years ago have morphed. We've moved from a single question in the 1980s—"Does collaborating make sense?"—to a new set of constructs based on the answer, "Yes. Collaboration can help agencies work together."

These new constructs include several lasting changes:

- *People expect seamless service across agencies and reduced barriers to making improvements in their lives and in their communities.* People bring a consumer's savvy to their service providers. Government agencies and nongovernmental organizations alike find that their clients are accelerating their access to services and demanding that the public sector behave and interact with them just as the business and private sector does. People once thought of as "clients" are thought of as "service consumers," "customers," and "partners."

- *Professionals are tired of limited collaboration success.* This happens when the lessons they learn and the improvements they birth fall by the wayside— because funding streams don't keep up with changes in best practices. Too often the hard work it takes to build product or programming together gets abandoned because the partner organizations will not change their budgets to account for the new ways to provide service.

- *Community leaders want responsive systems that don't duplicate effort or waste resources.* For instance, the Office of Homeland Security was established (in part) to streamline information exchange among law enforcement agencies. Welfare reform has been driven by elected leaders who know collaborative services are easier for clients to access and thus result in better, faster outcomes for families.

In the light of these challenges, what does a collaboration need to do to be successful? How can collaborations attend to these challenges without collapsing under their weight? How can real people in real time start and maintain a systems change effort?

Four Stages in Starting a Collaboration

During the 1980s, the Wilder Foundation conducted international research on collaborations. Researchers identified factors that influenced successful collaboration, including mutual trust, multiple layers of decision making, open communication, and a skilled convener. These factors were identified in *Collaboration: What Makes It Work.*[1]

Michael Winer and I incorporated this research into our own years of experience consulting with collaborations and subsequently created a model that describes the pattern of development in a collaborative effort. This model, outlined in detail in *Collaboration Handbook: Creating, Sustaining, and Enjoying the Journey*, has proved a worthy and reliable guide to identifying what's going on in any start-up collaboration and how to help collaborative efforts move along more quickly.

We defined collaboration as "a mutually beneficial and well-defined relationship entered into by two or more organizations to achieve results they are more likely to achieve together than alone."[2] We clarified the difference between cooperating, coordinating, and collaborating. Chapter One of this book reviews these ideas.

---

[1] Paul Mattessich, Marta Murray-Close, and Barbara Monsey, *Collaboration: What Makes It Work* (St. Paul, MN: Amherst H. Wilder Foundation, 2001).

[2] Michael Winer and Karen Ray, *Collaboration Handbook: Creating, Sustaining, and Enjoying the Journey* (St. Paul, MN: Amherst H. Wilder Foundation, 1994), 24.

ℐ

If you are just starting a collaboration or are participating in a relatively new one, work through the stages presented in *Collaboration Handbook*. By contrast, *The Nimble Collaboration* is intended for collaborations that have some basic experience and are ready to become nimble.

If you are just starting a collaboration or are participating in a relatively new one, work through the stages presented in *Collaboration Handbook*. By contrast, *The Nimble Collaboration* is intended for collaborations that have some basic experience and are ready to become nimble. This book does build on and incorporate the techniques suggested in *Collaboration Handbook*. Here is a brief review of the stages described therein.

Basically, collaborations grow up through stages of development. During Stage One, the member organizations build a shared vision and describe specific results they want from their work. This builds the confidence the group needs to begin Stage Two: ironing out conflicts and working through trust issues. When this work is well along, group members naturally begin to focus more on how they can be successful together, and they enter Stage Three: piloting projects, evaluating results, and getting the word out to the community at large. During Stage Four, member organizations assess how they work together and what, if anything, is next. Often at this point they realize that somehow the whole is bigger than the sum of its parts.

Enter the Nimble Collaboration

So why is collaborating so darn hard? There are many reasons. The four stages often unfold in fits and starts; some of the work in Stages One and Three often happens simultaneously; and some of the work in Stage Four needs to be considered while doing Stage One work.

The Nimble Collaboration anticipates this complexity. Sometimes partner organizations need to focus on process, sometimes on a task. Sometimes partners can see the big picture, the "aha, this is how my organization needs to be different in order to be effective." And sometimes, talking about change is the last thing partners need to do.

This new book suggests ways to fine-tune your existing collaboration's skills for handling complexity, and for making it more lean, more responsive, more flexible, and more productive—in a word, *nimble*. This book also explores what's next for collaborations. While *Collaboration Handbook* explained ways to start a collaboration, *The Nimble Collaboration* is about ways to make an existing collaboration more effective. If you are already working in a nonprofit collaboration that involves government agencies, nongovernmental organizations, community-building groups, nonprofits, law enforcement, education, health, housing, arts, social services, businesses, foundations—you name it—then this book is for you.

Readers familiar with *Collaboration Handbook*, or collaboration in general, will find some ideas repeated here. The reason is simple: Given the complexity of collaboration, participants overlook some of the most basic steps at start-up, and these oversights turn into problems later in the life of the collaboration. Thus, part of the process of becoming nimble involves a return to basics. But beyond that, existing collaborations have issues that differ from start-up collaborations:

- Continuously unproductive meetings
- Changing representatives at meetings
- Decisions that get made over and over again
- Partners who are not accountable to one another
- Conflicts that continue unresolved just under the surface
- Partnerships that die when the funding runs out
- Failure to embed best practices into the system

To become nimble, the collaboration needs to resolve these issues. And they *can* be resolved.

Nimble Collaboration Renews Institutions

Organizations that work together influence each other. Consider how your own role changes in the course of a collaboration: As you learn about what other organizations are doing, you rethink your own work. As you understand what the whole system looks like, you rethink your organization's place in the system. Collaboration is the art of gracefully influencing others, and being influenced by them. You change your organization—that is, you renew it—through these influences. Mutual accomplishment and mutual organizational renewal are at the very heart of collaboration. While the *goal* of collaboration is not organizational renewal, such renewal is the inevitable (and happy) outcome of almost all successful collaborations.

Many organizations do not understand this inherent result of being part of a collaboration. Often, when your organization becomes a partner in a collaboration, you expect to change some other organization, or some system or problem other than your own organization. When you create a nimble collaboration, you change your operations, programs, and services. You stop thinking of the people you serve in terms of their experience with you; instead, you think of them in terms of their experience with the system. You influence other agencies to change, and you accept the feedback about changes you need to make. You change your financing and budgets to reflect what you learn about best practices and customer success. You look different in three years from how you looked at the start of the collaboration.

Many collaborations avoid this hard truth. They run the collaboration as a "special project" parallel to their individual organizations' regular programming, never making the deep investments in organization renewal that the collaboration results suggest. They forget the reason they're knee-deep in all the meetings and work: to improve the system for customers, users, clients, staff, and all other stakeholders. These organizations miss an extraordinary opportunity to renew themselves.

i

When you create a nimble collaboration, you change your operations, programs, and services. You stop thinking of the people you serve in terms of their experience with you; instead, you think of them in terms of their experience with the system. . . .You look different in three years from how you looked at the start of the collaboration.

Paradoxically, although a lot of time is spent meeting with other organizations, much of collaboration is an internal affair involving the organization's examination of itself. Each participating organization can reinvigorate itself by updating programs or promoting best practices in its products and services in light of what it has learned about the whole system. Many organizations sit down at the collaboration meeting table as a partner without doing the internal, private work back in their own offices. These organizations have not grasped the fact that to accomplish the goals of the collaboration, they will need to make some internal changes—that collaboration involves mutual institutional renewal.

What does the nimble collaboration do if one of the partners is not doing its internal work? The collaboration puts the problem on the agenda by calling for discussion from each of the partners about the progress of their agency's reinvention. Institutional renewal cannot take place in an atmosphere of secrecy. In a nimble collaboration partners talk to each other about successes, stumbling blocks, doubts, and fears. Then they proceed with the important work of making each agency the best it can be for consumers. This book suggests many tactics you can use to enliven the discussion about reinvention.

Use Three Strategies to Become Nimble

The nimble collaboration moves quickly and responds to changing environments as participants

- Focus on *results*
- Shape *relationships*
- Structure for *resilience*

Use of these essential strategies predicts the difference between success and business as usual. They offer the most direct route to turn a cumbersome collaboration into a nimble collaboration.

Focus on results

Nimble collaborations revolve around the results participants want to achieve.[3] Partners need to know whether all the member organizations embrace the desired results as doable and important. As you and your partners discuss desired results, you become more certain about exactly how to produce them. Accountability gets spelled out, and you know who is responsible for what piece of the work. Partners can agree on a work plan, develop trusting relationships, and design a resilient structure.

---

[3] Collaborating *only* because the funder said to do it is misguided. Funders can prompt and facilitate collaboration, but when the focus is on meeting funding mandates rather than on producing results, the collaboration faces trouble.

When you and other members of your collaboration—the *agency representatives*—have agreed on the collaboration's intended results, the real work is just beginning. Each agency representative participating in the collaboration must champion these intentions back inside his or her own organization. The collaboration's statements of results—ranging from vision statements to month-by-month work plans—will make it clear to your peers and boss "back home" exactly what the collaboration wants to achieve, and what that means to your everyday work.

Chapter One explores the different levels of results that collaborations produce and explains how to define them.

Shape relationships

If your agency is a member of a collaboration, then your agency has in essence agreed to enter into relationships with the other member agencies. As in any relationship, trust is the key, and wise partners carry out action plans designed to build trust among organizations.

As you will read in Chapter Two, self-interest and trust are two sides of the same coin. Relationships can withstand difficulties only when partners know each other. Clarity about what members expect of each other and their roles is crucial. Specific communications processes can either build trust and reinforce roles or destroy both, so these processes are addressed in Chapter Two as well.

Structure for resilience

The word *nimble* implies responsiveness, an ability to change as circumstances change. Collaborations use complex ideas to resolve complex problems. The challenges are complicated and the conditions often fluctuate. Resiliency implies that the partners move and shift to accommodate circumstances they cannot control. At the same time, partners retain the core of the collaboration's mission. This requires a structure that can flex without breaking—without losing its bead on the primary purpose of the work. Resilient structure is the subject of Chapter Three.

Apply These Strategies to Two Types of Collaboration

When asked why an organization has joined a collaborative effort, its representatives will often say, "It's the right thing to do," "It's part of our mission," "It will help us innovate," or "We need to find ways to do more with what we have on hand." These attitudes reveal important questions about the goal of collaborating. Is it to build something new? Is it to create a new product, place, or service to fill a gap? Is it to eliminate duplication and fragmentation within the system? Is the goal to apply many approaches to resolve some complex problem?

The answers to these questions usually fall into two categories: Organizations often collaborate (1) to integrate services; or (2) to resolve complex issues. Part II of this book explores these two common types of collaboration. It offers examples to show how these collaborations can become nimble using the strategies of results, relationships, and resilience. While the particulars in the examples may be unfamiliar to you, the circumstances that befuddle them are familiar to most collaborations. The answers these collaborations have come up with are instructive.

Collaborate to integrate services

Collaborations to integrate services occur most frequently in education, housing, health care, recreation, the arts, law enforcement, and social services. Many professions are innovating the way they interact with consumers and the way they create outcomes. Collaborations to integrate services redesign the way work is done and demand different activities from individual professionals and organizations.

For instance, in social services there are initiatives to provide "wrap-around services," "unified case management," and "technology-centered assessments." Recently, in a central states collaboration, members stopped their usual practice of assembling documents from different agencies into a "family file." They had been doing this to share a client's "treatment plan." Instead, they started meeting as a team with the family to plan *in concert* how to help that family. This is service integration. The collaboration partners changed data-privacy protocols, altered social workers' schedules so they could attend evening family meetings, and changed standard operating procedures within individual agencies. They used a collaborative process to achieve these monumental changes, because the process had a better chance of getting everyone to buy into the changes. The collaboration resulted in giving families more power to develop plans they *believed in*—and thus were more likely to succeed at. Chapter Four looks closely at an initiative of this type.

The same principles apply no matter what kind of service to consumers you are bettering. In Florida, municipal housing development officers are working with senior citizen groups, ecologists, physicians, and law enforcement to create housing subdivisions that meld the services of health, safety, education, and citizenship into housing.

Chapter Four describes ways to succeed as you collaborate to redesign and integrate product and service delivery.

Collaborate to resolve complex issues

Some collaborations focus on multiple approaches to address complex community issues. Promoting sustainable agriculture, eliminating drug addiction, or increasing kids' exposure to the arts in school are the missions of complex collaborations in communities across the United States. The reason for multiple approaches is that such problems and visions cannot be achieved without many changes across many systems. For instance:

> The Centers for Disease Control and Prevention determined that communities' haphazard approach to HIV/AIDS was undermining efforts to eradicate the disease. The center offered financial support to communities willing to pull together all the organizations and groups fighting HIV/AIDS to jointly plan for prevention and education activities. In these collaborations, consumers, public health agencies, hospitals and doctors, community groups, and nongovernmental organizations have acknowledged that they will be working together for at least a dozen years in order to have a big impact on the health of their communities.

Many communities are facing these kinds of difficult issues head on. They respond by collaborating to plan and implement many different activities from many different resources to address the issues. Consider this example:

> Agencies in a metropolitan community in Minnesota were worried. They all served meals and provided food to hungry people, and they all asked for funding from a handful of local churches and foundations. But their individual funding applications confused givers because the numbers they used varied widely. Some agencies reported many more hungry people living in the community than others; some agencies seemed to feed families of four on $10 a meal, and others spent $25. Which of these vastly different numbers represented the real picture?

> The agencies' executive directors decided to collaborate to produce numbers that made sense to everyone in the community. Some of the results they wanted from their collaboration were (1) to gather data about hungry people and their needs in the same way and (2) to count costs for feeding people in a parallel fashion. This parallel goal implementation required a collaborative approach. The agencies had to exchange detailed information and create policies in conjunction with one another.

The remarkable thing about these collaborations is sheer numbers—the number of people involved, the number of agencies that are collaborating, and the number of years the community expects to stay engaged in the collaboration. This kind of collaboration requires special attributes to succeed. Look to Chapter Five for some ideas.

Get the Most from This Book

While Part I (Chapters One–Three) explains the guiding strategies of nimble collaboration, Part II (Chapters Four and Five) walks you through real-life applications of these ideas. Whatever collaboration you're in, ideas in these stories can help you solve a problem you're experiencing.

At the end of Chapter Three is a special section on how to write the various documents that bind partners together on paper. These templates can help you infuse your collaboration with the three Rs—results, relationships, and resilience.

Remember that not every part of your collaboration can be documented. For many collaborations, the simple act of talking about roles, responsibilities, and decision making is more important than the steps of documentation. During early stages of development, such discussion builds trust as agency representatives share and clarify expectations. Later on, you and your partners will want a more formal declaration of the relationship that exists among you and the ways you will govern yourselves. This can happen, for example, when work planning seriously begins (such as submitting a grant application) or when beginning the implementation phase of a long-term project.

Many of the other sample documents in this book are actual documents being used in collaborations or compilations of actual documents. Feel free to use these as templates for your own work.

Finally, remember that *nothing in this book should be perceived as legal counsel.* If your collaboration requires legal documentation, seek professional legal advice. However, you can use this book to draft paragraphs or ideas you want to be sure to include in your contracts. Collaborations are new to many attorneys, so you will want to be clear about what you want, and not be led by their more traditional approaches.

This book can help your collaboration devise ways to address problems triumphantly. If you have not yet agreed on the ways in which you will make decisions, resolve conflict, or assign responsibilities, then this book is a useful guide for you. If you have structure or decision-making issues, or need to document your agreements, then this book can provide many useful tips.

Throughout this book you'll find sidebars—samples, examples, case histories, and useful techniques that enhance the main text. These extra elements present a rich treasury of "how-tos" based on my twenty years of experience consulting with real people in real collaborations across the United States. Some of these stories are true, and some are composites based on several collaborations. Each story illustrates a key point. For deeper background on the issues involved in nimble collaboration, dig into the list of selected readings in Appendix B.

You'll also find occasional "action steps." These are steps a collaboration can take to make itself more nimble. You'll know these by the name, *Action Step*, and by the icon of Jack being nimble, jumping over the candlestick. For reference, these action steps are collected in a chart that falls between Parts I and II (pages 76–77).

Collaborating nimbly is a useful, exciting way to accomplish goals. In these pages may you find the answers you need to get results, build relationships, and resiliently pursue your vision.

PART I

To Become Nimble, Focus on Results, Relationships, and Resilience

"Nimble collaboration" is not an oxymoron. It *is* possible to be in a collaboration and move deftly to accomplish tasks. But such behavior is not automatic. Attention to three overarching strategies—focusing on results, shaping relationships, and structuring for resilience—helps naturally cumbersome collaborations operate with surprising agility. Chapters One, Two, and Three provide information and actions to help your collaboration adopt these strategies and, in the process, become nimble.

Chapter One

Focus on Results

Albert Einstein said, "I know why everyone loves to chop wood. One immediately sees the results." *Focusing on results* is one of the three primary strategies a nimble collaboration employs. Gaining clarity about results will help you and your partners focus on the rewards of doing this work.

Results are the solid platform that allows the partnership to perform flexibly and deftly. Nimble collaboration calls on you to specify the results of your collaboration by stating your

- Premise
- Promise
- Mission
- Vision
- Outcomes
- Evaluation criteria
- Work plan

This chapter discusses each of these elements in turn and offers tips for using them to make a collaboration nimble.

Consider Your Premise

"I thought we were just going to implement an idea we got some grant money for. I didn't expect it to be so complicated!" This is a common complaint, frequently heard at collaboration meetings. It's easy to misunderstand the intentions of others when the word *collaboration* is thrown about haphazardly.

The problem is that people use *coordinating, cooperating,* and *collaborating* as interchangeable words. Actually, these are distinct processes that demand more or less of the partners involved. If coordinating, cooperating, and collaborating were laid out on a continuum that describes how complicated the work is, collaborating would be the most complicated. This is because the premise of collaboration is that at least two organizations must be interdependently involved in addressing an issue. When organizations collaborate, they are agreeing to work on a complex situation where "what to do" and "how to do it" are not easily answered. Figure 1: Cooperation, Coordination, and Collaboration, page 19, helps differentiate the three types of work.

Once the organizations that want to work together on a problem have explored their premise options, they can wisely assess their capacity for collaboration and the potential for success. They may also realize that some less intense process—cooperation or coordination—is all that's needed.

Coordination

Coordinating is the least intense way of working together, but it has enormous impact when intentionally employed. When your agency coordinates with another, you exchange information, and you may decide to use the information to improve your own services. Examples of coordination include

- Putting your organization's name on United Way campaign literature during a funding drive
- Cosponsoring a training event for professionals
- Listing information about your organization in a directory or consumer guide

Just as coordinates on a map provide scale and an easy way to see where you stand, this level of working together allows a system or a set of consumers to understand your organization in relation to other organizations.

Often coordinating involves short-term or relatively uncomplicated tasks. In such cases, it is easy for the coordinating partners to predict how much risk each will assume. A simple example: A municipal office of economic development and the three biggest employers in town conduct a job fair to attract potential employees to the town. The advertising brochure lists all three organizations, their logos, and separate contact information. The fair is held for free at city hall, and the businesses buy advertising in nearby towns. This coordinated activity is productive and straightforward, and the inherent risks and challenges are easy for each organization to anticipate and resolve.

Cooperation

Cooperating ratchets up the intensity of the working relationship. When organizations cooperate, often the project itself is more complicated than in coordination. Organizations contribute more resources to the task. More planning time is required to make the task successful. Partners exchange more detailed information about their budgets, work plans, funders, and so on. Organizations risk more when they cooperate because their reputations get deeply tied to those of their partners.

Often a cooperative effort is funded by a grant, and the request for a proposal uses the word *collaborate*. In reality, the granters are simply asking for you to cooperate to get a specific task accomplished. Cooperating is a smart way to get things done. It is also less complicated than collaboration, allowing you to skip some of the processes described in this book.

Co-location of services is often a great example of a cooperative effort masquerading as collaboration. Co-location means moving all or part of your office and programs to a site shared by similar offices and programs. This can be a valuable and productive move, for instance, to improve accessibility for clients and save money for the organizations. But co-location that does not involve changing the way the organizations work together to serve customers is not really a collaborative effort.

Collaboration

Consider the co-location example above. Suppose that the boss of Agency One says this to the boss of Agency Two: "After we move into the building together, we need to share information about some clients because we could serve them better." Then Boss Two says, "That's true, and we're getting pressure from our funders to make our services more accessible. Do you think we should have a common intake form?" Boss One says, "Let's try to. And let's see what other changes we need to make to improve access."

In this case, the agencies are starting a collaboration. Besides sharing office space, they may choose to share a single intake worker, develop a common intake form with uniform data-privacy and data-sharing protocol, link computer systems for common databases, and conduct joint staff training. These tasks require long discussions with staff, clients, funders, and the community. When organizations grapple first with an issue (such as "seamless" service) and then decide what tasks the partners should do together, they are probably entering a collaboration.

Collaboration is the most intense way organizations work together while maintaining separate identities. It is not better or worse than cooperating or coordinating; it is simply

Collaboration mystery revealed

Collaboration is an act of bravery. Some people or organizations treat collaboration as business as usual, but it's not. You'll know you're collaborating when you see that you must ask another agency to leave the collaboration if all it wants is access to the grant money. Shaping relationships with honesty and directness requires a degree of courage beyond what's necessary for simply co-operating or coordinating.

the most intense commitment an organization can make to changing a system. When collaborating, organizations agree to influence—and be influenced by—each other.

The premise of this partnership is that individual agencies agree to change their programming and budgets to help create a better system of services for constituents. Collaboration means the participating organizations will change.

When you collaborate, you work with everyone who is part of the system, including those agencies that have made you uncomfortable in the past. You shape relationships that will serve you as the collaboration does long-range and difficult work.

Collaboration is not always the best way to do work together. In many instances a cooperative or coordinated effort is the best way to work together. Either of these can be a wise change strategy that is less complicated than collaboration, demands less of organizations, and can show results more quickly. If you are in a group that's called a collaboration but are engaged in a cooperative or a coordinated effort, that's great. You don't need complicated instructions or sophisticated agreements. Just go out and do your work!

Action Step

At the next meeting of collaborative partners, decide which premise best describes your current activities: coordination, cooperation, or collaboration. Recognizing that you are cooperating or coordinating instead of collaborating is *not* a disadvantage. It simply helps the group better understand and anticipate the challenges, the amount of work to do, and the risks of that joint work.

Consider Your Promise

Once organizations have determined that the *premise* of their work together is to collaborate (to achieve some goal interdependently that an agency cannot achieve alone), then the collaboration can consider its *promise*.

A collaboration is frequently started and defined by circumstances. A law is changed, for instance, or a foundation funds an initiative. Often, somebody *outside* the collaboration's community says, "You can do a better job than you're currently doing." This is how many welfare reform collaborations were born. Similarly, foundations have seen systems change successfully when collaborations work on problems, so they sometimes offer grant money for collaborative "initiatives."

Other collaborations are birthed *inside* the community. They grow from the grass roots, energized by the community's demand for better service or better lifestyle. Many economic development and housing collaborations have come from grassroots demands for better communities and from the leaders who listen to them.[4]

---

4   Thanks to Arthur Himmelman for the concept of "betterment" and "empowerment" in collaborations, which is related to the concept of whether the driving force behind the collaboration is external or internal, as presented in "Communities Working Collaboratively for a Change," *Resolving Conflict: Strategies for Local Government* (Washington, D.C: International City/County Management Association, 1994).

Figure 1: Cooperation, Coordination, and Collaboration
A Table Describing the Elements of Each[5]

Essential Elements	Cooperation	Coordination	Collaboration
Vision and Relationships	• Basis for cooperation is usually between individuals but may be mandated by a third party • Organizational missions and goals are not taken into account • Interaction is on an as needed basis, may last indefinitely	• Individual relationships are supported by the organizations they represent • Missions and goals of the individual organizations are reviewed for compatibility • Interaction is usually around one specific project or task of definable length	• Commitment of the organizations and their leaders is fully behind their representatives • Common, new mission and goals are created • One or more projects are undertaken for longer-term results
Structure, Responsibilities, and Communication	• Relationships are informal; each organization functions separately • No joint planning is required • Information is conveyed as needed	• Organizations involved take on needed roles, but function relatively independently of each other • Some project-specific planning is required • Communication roles are established and definite channels are created for interaction	• New organizational structure and/or clearly defined and inter-related roles that constitute a formal division of labor are created • More comprehensive planning is required that includes developing joint strategies and measuring success in terms of impact on the needs of those served • Beyond communication roles and channels for interaction, many "levels" of communication are created as clear information is a keystone of success
Authority and Accountability	• Authority rests solely with individual organizations • Leadership is unilateral and control is central • All authority and accountability rests with the individual organization which acts independently	• Authority rests with the individual organizations, but there is coordination among participants • Some sharing of leadership and control • There is some shared risk, but most of the authority and accountability falls to the individual organizations	• Authority is determined by the collaboration to balance ownership by the individual organizations with expediency to accomplish purpose • Leadership is dispersed, and control is shared and mutual • Equal risk is shared by all organizations in the collaboration
Resources and Rewards	• Resources (staff time, dollars, and capabilities) are separate, serving the individual organization's needs	• Resources are acknowledged and can be made available to others for a specific project • Rewards are mutually acknowledged	• Resources are pooled or jointly secured for a longer-term effort that is managed by the collaborative structure • Organizations share in the products; more is accomplished jointly than could have been individually

[5] Mattessich, Murray-Close, and Monsey, *Collaboration: What Makes It Work*, 61. Used with permission.

The circumstances surrounding the beginning of your collaboration, whether influenced by outsiders or insiders to your business, offer an implicit *promise*. Illuminating this promise helps your collaboration get clear about the work it is doing.

As an example, imagine a collaboration's purpose is to increase parents' participation in classroom activities. Most collaborations just get busy planning and carrying out tasks. They develop marketing materials to attract parents to classrooms, and design training activities for teachers who work with parents. Before getting busy with all these activities, the nimble collaboration asks, "Who will be judging our success? Is this something parents have asked for, so we must think about measuring our success in terms parents will understand? Or is this a new law from the state legislature? Must we plan our work to account for a bureaucratic reporting system?" Understanding *who* is being promised *what* lets the nimble collaboration pay attention to important details. If teachers asked for help getting parents to the classroom, then more money and work may be needed to attract parents. However, if this is a newly mandated law, then more money and work may be needed to convince teachers that involving parents will be helpful to them, not just more work for them.

Action Step

Ask, "Who will be judging our success? Will the collaboration be judged by legislators who passed a new law, a foundation that offered grant money, the customers we serve, or the leaders of our own organizations?" Decide what **results** you are promising to whom, and write them down. The strongest collaborations weave this promise into their vision or mission statements.

State Your Mission

A collaboration's mission is the most general statement of its desired results—a statement of what benefit the collaboration will provide for which community. It answers questions such as *So what?* and *Why bother to try this at all?* Regardless of circumstances, collaborations usually begin among people who meet and talk and ask, *Is this a good idea?* The answers are summed in a mission statement.[6] Here are two examples:

> A collaboration to reduce substance abuse among teens wrote its mission as: "Youth are empowered to choose a drug-free lifestyle."

> A collaboration that dealt with the employment of developmentally disabled adults wrote: "Developmentally disabled adults in our town are employed in a manner that is personally meaningful to them."

---

[6] For advice on mission and vision statements and how to write them, see Emil Angelica, *The Wilder Nonprofit Field Guide to Crafting Effective Mission and Vision Statements* (St. Paul, MN: Amherst H. Wilder Foundation, 2001).

The mission statement is stable. It is a placeholder for the participating organizations' roles in the collaboration. The collaboration's mission statement has room for the separate mission statements of participating agencies. It may expand and contract over time, but the basic thrust remains.

As your collaboration shapes its mission, it faces one of the chief consternations of collaboration: sorting (and reconciling) what it wants to do, what funders want it to do, and what each partner wants it to do. Nimble collaborations prepare for the demands that will probably come their way.

Perhaps someone has successfully applied for a grant, or a federal office has released money to one partner to pass through to other partners. Many collaborations struggle when a partner (or two!) shows up "in order to get the money." Sometimes a board or a boss will tell a middle manager, "You show up as our representative in that collaboration and make sure we don't lose any revenue on this thing."

A solution is to be deliberate, not directed. Don't be directed by others' reactions or anxieties. The next step is for the collaboration to be deliberate about what it wants *as a collaboration.*

This deliberation can involve many questions. Does the collaboration want to do a task and get it done in one year? Does it want to change a system, for instance, by reducing duplication or knitting together a continuum of services? Does it want to impact a key issue or move an entire community toward some lifestyle improvement? What's really in it for each member and for the group? What does each agency think is a reasonable mission?

Answering questions like these leads to describing the collaboration's mission. Those answers will help the collaborative partners clarify the kind of results they are seeking.

 A true fable . . .New members mean mission massage

The school principal walked into the meeting room, took stock of the seating arrangements, and found a chair at the table. The meeting began soon after, and the facilitator asked people to introduce themselves. When it was the principal's turn, she said, "My name is Sue Smith, and I'm principal of Garden High School. I don't know why I'm here. The superintendent called me and said I should attend these meetings." Some people looked chagrined, but the meeting facilitator was relaxed. He knew that they were entering the first round of exploring their promise for working together. Getting the schools to the table was a big achievement. The original mission and vision for the collaboration would have to be massaged in order to learn what the schools had to offer, and to make the effort worthwhile for the schools.

State Your Vision

A vision statement describes the journey the collaborating organizations take over the years to fulfill their mission. A vision statement focuses the work and may refer to the promise and mission of the collaboration. While mission statements are usually only one or two sentences, vision statements may need more words as they paint a picture of the desired results after three to ten years' work by the collaboration.

To distinguish vision and mission, think of the vision as the selling point that attracts other organizations to the collaboration; in turn, the mission statement is a place-holder for organizations' roles in the collaboration. (Advertisers speak in terms of "selling the sizzle, not the steak." The vision is the sizzle—the exciting future your collaboration promises. The mission is the steak—the substance of what you do.)

As members are added to the meeting table, the vision for the collaboration expands or contracts. The vision for the collaboration is a guiding desire, an ideal end to a lot of work.

> For the mission statement, "Youth are empowered to choose a drug-free lifestyle," the vision statement could be: "We will build a web of recreational activities that build on preteens' strengths. Within five years, most young people in our community will have participated in our programs, and will be making positive choices that reduce their risk of alcohol and other drug use."

> For the mission statement, "Developmentally disabled adults in our town are employed in a manner that is personally meaningful to them," the vision statement could be: "We will collaborate to provide employment readiness training and on-the-job services to adults with developmental disabilities. Within ten years, as a result of our work, most developmentally disabled adults in our community will be employed in ways that benefit them and their employers. Our community will be a national model."

Notice that these mission and vision combinations do not describe specific actions. Specific descriptions belong in the collaboration's work plan, and in the work plans of each home agency. Rather, the mission and vision form the broad goal and the bright future that will spur the many plans, programs, and activities.

Nimble collaborations revisit the vision statement when they complete an evaluation cycle—for instance, at the end of the first year.

Action Step

Plan time to revisit the collaboration mission statement and vision statement whenever

- New partners are added
- Evaluation cycles are completed
- Questions about the direction of the collaboration surface

State Your Desired Results as Outcomes

Mission and vision statements are the broadest ways to describe the results you want. As important as they are for setting direction and engaging organization partners effectively, it is in stating outcomes that the rubber hits the road. Outcome statements describe in detail how the collaboration will know when it has accomplished its vision and mission. Most often, outcomes are statements of measurable results.

Outcome statements describe what has happened to people, products, and problems as a result of all the efforts undertaken by the collaborating partners. Outcome statements drive everyday decisions and offer benchmarks of success.

For instance, consider the mission statement, "Youth are empowered to choose a drug-free lifestyle," and its associated vision statement, "We will build a web of recreational activities that build on preteens' strengths. Within five years, most young people in our community will have participated in our programs, and will be making positive choices that reduce their risk of alcohol and other drug use." Outcome statements might include

- "One hundred percent of the youth engaged in our programs who have never used drugs report that they do not want to start drug use.

- "Seventy-five percent of the youth engaged in our programs who have used drugs report reduced incidence of drug use.

- "Every preteen in our town is within walking distance of a supervised, neighborhood-based, after-school recreation site."

Nimble collaborations use these outcome statements as guides through every decision-making process. Some collaborations print them on easel chart paper and laminate them, so the outcome statements can be hung up at every meeting. When partners are struggling over a decision, they can turn to the outcome statements and ask, "How will this suggested solution help us reach these results?"

Action Step

Write outcome statements that will bring you close to your mission and vision. Use these statements actively during your meetings and for making decisions.

State Your Evaluation Criteria

Evaluation criteria are numeric or qualitative indicators, attached to specific actions, that show whether the collaboration's stated outcomes are being attained. Nowadays, most funders are interested in measurements of real change, such as "truancy among eleven-year-olds who participated in this program has dropped 50 percent, while truancy rates remain unchanged among nonparticipants." Evaluation criteria such as this help the collaboration build stronger and more customer-responsive activities during the next program year or work cycle.

Consider the example of the collaboration established to reduce substance abuse among teens. Its mission was "Youth are empowered to choose a drug-free lifestyle" and its vision was "We will build a web of recreational activities that build on pre-teens' strengths. Within five years, most young people in our community will have participated in our programs, and will be making positive choices that reduce their risk of alcohol and other drug use." Finally, its *outcomes* were

- "One hundred percent of the youth engaged in our programs who have never used drugs report that they do not want to start drug use.
- "Seventy-five percent of the youth engaged in our programs who have used drugs report reduced incidence of drug use.
- "Every preteen in our town is within walking distance of a supervised, neighborhood-based, after-school recreation site."

In search of true outcomes

Do your evaluation criteria measure input, output, or outcomes? Often, collaborations mistake input or output for outcomes—and thus they measure the wrong things.

Input for your collaboration consists of the resources (financial, human, intellectual, or other) that the partners put into the work of the collaboration. This might include the governance structure you've created, the staff you've employed, or the resources the partner organizations have put into the collaboration, such as money or programs.

Output for the collaboration consists of the work that gets done with those resources: such things as the number of clients seen, or the number of training programs offered. Collaborations often make the mistake of measuring output instead of outcome: "We're finding the federal funds for one hundred new affordable units of housing." Or "We're offering ten after-school programs." Or "Two hundred and fifty adults with substance abuse problems are receiving wrap-around services." These measurements let people know the collaboration is working, but they don't speak to the effects (the outcomes) of the work.

Outcome is the change that happens (or fails to happen, if the collaboration's work is unsuccessful) as a result of the input and output: Positive outcomes for the outputs described in the preceding paragraph would include "Sixty new affordable housing units have been built." Or "Test scores have improved 42 percent for kids who participate in the homework club." Or "Seventy-five percent of the adults with substance abuse problems who receive wrap-around services are still sober one year after completing their programs."

When your collaboration specifies the outcomes it wants to achieve, it should state clearly what changes will occur as a result of the inputs (resources) and outputs (work) the collaborative partners apply. These can be translated into specific, measurable evaluation criteria for the collaboration.

The evaluation might reflect the progress the collaboration has made toward these outcomes. Or, progress could be measured in many other ways, and each of its program activities could have specific evaluation criteria attached. Some possibilities include the following:

- "Pre- and post-attitude inventories of youth who have been involved in the collaboration's programs show improved ability to resist drug use. (Measures attitude change among participants, a goal of the program.)

- "Before and after maps of the community show that as a result of the collaboration's work, every young person is within a fifteen-minute walk of a recreational site. (Measures whether the collaboration has made its programs widely accessible.)

- "Evidence shows that all recreational sites offer programs based on the drug-resistance models implemented by the collaboration. (Measures whether the collaboration has met its goal of getting the program adopted at every recreational site.)

- "Survey results indicate that youth enjoyed the programs and that new participants are attending as a result of word-of-mouth advertising by current participants. (Measures the success of the program as being so enjoyable to youth that they encourage their friends to attend, thus involving more youth.)"

Action Step

Put a half-day retreat on the calendar for all the partners in the collaboration. Part of the time can be spent celebrating any positive evaluation of outcomes, and part of the time can be spent evaluating the collaboration effort itself.

Create Your Work Plan

When a collaboration has stated its mission, vision, outcomes, and evaluation criteria, it's finally time to talk about programs and activities—to write or revise the existing work plan.

The work plan can describe new programs and activities. It might identify target dates for changing services or describe how the new programs will be put in place. The work plan can also identify what existing programs will be modified. Programs and activities are owned and operated by individual organizations, and those organizations are expected to adjust them to build the best system for consumers and clients. This plan will affect the budgets of the organizations that are part of the collaboration, so setting out timetables can help the partner organizations plan ahead for the financial impact.

For many organizations involved in collaboration, a work plan typically includes *pilot projects*, *standard operating procedures*, and *directions to hire a coordinator* who oversees the day-to-day activity involved in collaboration. Unless approached consciously and carefully, each of these elements of a work plan can quickly derail your attempts at nimble collaboration. The next sections explain ways to avoid this fate.

Consider the perils of pilot projects

Many collaborations try out a project in a small way, often called "piloting" a project. For instance, rather than having a new intake form for all clients, you use a new intake form only for clients who want a particular cluster of services. If you and your partners find that the new form works well, then you can introduce it into all agencies for use by all clients.

Pilot projects can work, but they come with risks. A sure way to kill your agency's excitement to do things better is to run a pilot project along with the regular way to do work and never merge the two. Many collaborations identify (or develop) best practices, which then disappear from their organizations when the collaboration funding runs out.

There are other dangers to pilot projects. Staff members may pretend they really don't have to change behaviors. Administrators may ignore the budget implications of changing their procedures because the pilot is a grant project, not something that requires real change. Clients may suffer since truly useful changes never get implemented on a broad scale. The result is a deadly form of procrastinator's disease known as "running parallel systems": allowing the original, old-fashioned practices to continue to operate while the alternative system is working—and succeeding—as a pilot project.

The collaboration must decide. Do you really need a pilot to practice your results? Or is that an excuse to avoid doing the hard work you must do in order to succeed? The following example illustrates how one collaboration answered these questions.

> The consultant was excited. She left a meeting she had just facilitated and was sure that the great potential of this group was being realized. It was a small county in a western state where a collaborative strategy was at work. The social support organizations had experienced success in their initial efforts to work together to eliminate drug and alcohol abuse. They had the endorsement of other community organizations and basked in the support of the business community. They had initiated some neighborhood efforts that generated enthusiasm in the local foundation.

> Even the community's small size was an asset. The collaboration had the luxury of working with the police to identify the fifteen individuals and families who caused a large percentage of alcohol or drug-related police calls. It was their intention to do "unified case management" for these fifteen families as a pilot to more widespread service integration. The

facilitator was excited about the statements made by the caseworker from the treatment center. "We've got to stop talking about teaming up and really meet and get these clients into single treatment strategies that work," he said.

At the next meeting the facilitator assumed these joint case management meetings had taken place, but when she asked how they were going the partners looked at her blankly. Talking about having those meetings and actually beginning joint case management were two different things. Then and there, the facilitator organized the first joint case management meeting among four different providers.

One of the providers was upset. "But we're already doing joint treatment planning," she complained, "and I know because it's my job to collect everybody's treatment plan into one file!" A senior member of the collaboration took her aside to explain more completely what "joint case management" meant. Even over the din of other conversations the group could hear her excited voice when she caught on: "Oh! You mean we'd sit together with the client and devise one plan! Can we do that?" Yes, the group agreed enthusiastically, we can do that.

And they did. Alcohol and drug treatment was never the same for the professionals or their clients. No pilot project was needed. The change was simply made *now*.

Action Step

Be sure to include the following elements into your work plan if your collaboration is considering—or currently operates—a pilot project.

- *A rationale for the pilot project.* Do you need the pilot, or is it better to ask partners to change their programs immediately?
- *Criteria for success.* How will you know if the pilot project is working well?
- *An evaluation plan.* How will you get staff and consumer input? Who is responsible for the evaluation, when is it due, and when will you look at the evaluation and apply the criteria for success?
- *A deadline for expanding the pilot.* When will the pilot cease being a pilot and be applied to all appropriate work?

Embed change in standard operating procedures

Many collaborations have been funded to create innovative programs better suited to clients' needs. And many of these programs die as soon as the funding is over. "Why do good ideas and great performance get ignored by the funders?" a literacy teacher moaned. "We've really made a difference in the way parents pay attention to their kids' reading skills. Why is the foundation discontinuing funding?"

Most foundation and government funding initiatives are designed to be "seed money" or experimental money, especially when they involve collaborative efforts. These resources are trying to help systems change, to adopt best practices. Problems arise—and programs die—when actions are not taken to fully embed the changes in the system. Instead, the systems often don't "adopt" anything. They run parallel programs—for instance, the traditional adult basic education literacy programs are run alongside the new family-oriented literacy efforts. Once the grant money is in the bank, the already overburdened executive director or school superintendent can forget (quite understandably) about the program, often just thankful for the extra resources. As a result, their organizations don't thoughtfully design future budgets that fuel the changes in operating procedures necessary to absorb the new program. Or they worry and try to find "additional" funds to make the program permanent, forgetting that something they're already doing will have to stop in order to make way for the new.

Some collaborations are experiencing enormous success by immersing themselves in the new system. The easiest way to do this permanently is to change each member agency's standard operating procedures.

Standard operating procedures (SOPs) are an agency's internal directions to its workers that tell them how to carry out a job. Sometimes SOPs are included in job descriptions or employee manuals. As your collaboration finds answers and reinvents ways to do business, each member agency's SOPs can change so that the best practices are cemented into place. As the following example indicates, such changes can have an impact even if they're small.

In 1998 in Duluth, Minnesota, four different organizations provided meals for hungry people: CHUM, a church-based organization; the Salvation Army; the Union Gospel Mission; and a nonprofit organization named Damiano. As this group built its collaboration, the organizations wanted to take better advantage of fresh fruit that occasionally was made available to one of them. At the time this group started together, the organization that received the fruit accepted or declined the offer based solely on

Collaboration mystery revealed

You can embed changes in the system by changing the standard operating procedures (SOPs) that drive the system. The following are snippets from actual agency SOPs that reflect the agreements made by the collaboration the agency is working with.

Our agency no longer provides interpreters for deaf clients. When you are working for a deaf client, contact the ABC agency at 555-5555 and request an interpreter. After you use an interpreter's services, you will fill out that interpreter's billing form.

All new employees attend interagency training on seamless customer service. That training is offered three times a year by the Community College. Contact the city clerk at 555-5555. Your supervisor must receive your proof of attendance no later than six months after your first day of work.

When a treatment bed opens, phone the information to the lead worker in the Unified Case Management Team. You must phone her with information on the open bed before you leave your shift. The lead worker is Jane Doe at the Walk-In Center on High Street, and her phone number is 555-5555.

Simple, but effective. Changing SOPs changes organizations, and these organizations often find renewed vigor. Such institutional renewal is the outcome of collaboration.

its own needs. During a meeting the partners devised a plan that made the fruit available to all of the organizations so it would never go to waste.

At the next meeting, members of each organization arrived with a page out of their employee handbook, or SOPs, that incorporated this new procedure into the job. Each partner had enough copies of the document for the rest of the group so that everyone had a record of who changed what and how. They left the meeting knowing they had changed the system successfully, even if it was a small change.[7]

Changing SOPs is one way partners can show that the change has taken place inside their home organizations and make sure the next person that gets the job learns the right processes. Then the collaboration isn't relying on specific individuals to keep the collaboration on the right track.

Action Step

Consider which best practices are ready to be incorporated as standard operating procedures within each partner agency. Set a deadline for meeting to share these changes in SOPs among members of the collaboration.

Consider whether or not to hire a coordinator

In the beginning of a collaboration, the work can seem overwhelming. Hiring someone to be the collaboration coordinator makes great sense. Most foundation-funded collaborations (and many state- and federally-funded collaborations) authorize part of the grant for hiring a collaboration coordinator. Coordinators allow collaboration members to pay attention to the rest of the work and to champion the efforts of the collaboration back in their own offices, which is often a great deal of work in itself.

In some cases a collaboration will always use a coordinator: in urban settings where many partners and lots of activities are under way, for instance, or when the collaboration believes it may need to be in place for years in order to achieve its desired results.

If a collaboration wants to use a coordinator effectively, it might consider some innovative job descriptions. Much of a coordinator's job is clerical—sending out meeting notices and documents. On the other hand, a collaboration might want someone to facilitate meetings or look for funding opportunities. Getting this broad skill set in one person can be difficult. Perhaps clerical work can be assigned to a partner organization that has the resources to handle it, and a grantwriter can be hired on a consulting basis to help with funding. Then the coordinator's job description can be more focused and carefully constructed to avoid pitfalls.

The smaller and more focused the collaborative effort, the less need there may be for a full-time, full-term coordinator. There are many pitfalls to the coordinator's role.

---

[7] The author is grateful to these organizations for permission to cite their success.

In fact, as the collaboration matures, the coordinator can become an unwitting barrier to deft moves and nimble responsiveness by the partners.

To begin, coordinators can be seduced into difficult or inappropriate roles, such as conflict mediator, resource distributor, and nag (calling people to remind them of meetings or tasks that were supposed to be completed by a certain date). In addition, coordinators are usually competent initiators who will take on more and more duties in an effort to be sure the collaboration works. Unwittingly, they are reinforcing the myth that the coordinator is the person who does most of the work of the collaboration, so the collaboration partners themselves avoid the work they must engage in to be successful. This is a deadly perspective. Consider the perils of Pauline in the following collaboration:

> Roughly one dozen agencies shaped Health Collaboration in an urban community on the East Coast. These agencies were nonprofit or grassroots organizations, frequently staffed with an executive director and one or two other part-time people. Members included a variety of well-known volunteer-heavy organizations. Two executive directors realized everyone could save money if they shared back-office expenses, such as telephone, computers, and duplication. After more than a year's meetings, the executive directors of all the agencies got approval from their boards to rent space together.

> In order to help with expenses, and to get more needed "person power," the partners applied for and won a grant to hire a coordinator and pay for the moving expenses for each agency. They hired Pauline, a self-starter with a lot of energy and obvious talents for planning.

> Pauline had quite a time going from meeting to meeting of each agency's board and each agency's staff as she collected information and set priorities for choosing office space to lease. Every time she found a location that met most of the criteria, somebody seemed to be opposed to that spot and she'd start all over again. After a draining two years, the group approved of an old, rehabilitated building, and she and realtors started negotiating leases for each of the partners. Everyone was so pleased with the job she was doing that they applied for a different grant to pay her to be the executive director of the collaboration.

> After the honeymoon period Pauline predicted would follow the relocation, conflicts began to emerge—among some executive directors who had been fighting all along, to be sure, but also among middle-level administrators, such as program directors. Pauline's days seemed to be spent mediating disagreements about "overuse" by one agency of the computer modem telephone line or about overlong meetings in the conference room.

One day as Pauline was leaving the office at her usual time (6:30 p.m.), she began experiencing chest pains. Fortunately someone else was still in the building and called 911. Six weeks later, Pauline had recovered from her stress-induced irregular heartbeat. She was back at work full time, and not a moment too soon. During her absence several important deadlines had been missed, including an opportunity to renegotiate rent rates and a deadline for submitting a grant report. These funders subsequently refused to consider another application from Health Collaboration.

Remember, a collaboration is not a grant project. Consider it a paid opportunity to change your programs and your budget to improve a community or give customers a better product. A coordinator should support partners who are trying to change the system in some way. The partners themselves remain the primary workers on the project. If you or your agency has come to the collaboration table to access grant money, and if you believe the collaboration coordinator is responsible for the success of the grant, you are misinterpreting the role of coordinator.

Most funders, especially private foundations, will not continue to support a coordinator position indefinitely. If your collaboration has hired or plans to hire a coordinator, include in your work plan a specific way in which the collaboration will be weaned off the coordinator function, should that function no longer be needed.

Collaboration mystery revealed

If you are a collaboration coordinator and your boss or your partners refer to your work as "that special project" or "your project," then they are not seeing your role or their own role correctly. Collaboration is *not* a "project"; it is a strategy for changing the way partners do business. You are not coordinating a special project. You are relieving people of some of the daily chores of collaboration so they can have more time to make changes inside their agencies.

Common tasks that are gradually absorbed by members themselves include

- Convene meetings, chair them, publish agendas ahead of time, and write and distribute meeting summaries.
- Hold people accountable for quality. Ensure that those responsible for carrying out specific tasks on the work plan are doing so.
- Develop a "resource-hunt" mentality in all work to uncover new resources. Seek out new partners and explore the system for opportunities for support.
- Nurture relationships among members and with other entities as appropriate. Implement a communications plan to accomplish this. (More on this in Chapter Two.)
- Provide and manage the office space and support, such as computers and phones.
- Supervise and evaluate any staff and subcontractors hired by the collaboration.

A collaboration currently using a coordinator can follow a three-year plan to reduce dependence on that position. For the first year, eliminate only grantwriting responsibilities from your coordinator's job description. In the second year, reduce your coordinator's position to one-quarter time. This person remains primarily responsible for following up on task completion, documenting meetings, and preparing reports. Simultaneously, increase collaboration partners' accountability for communications, resource hunting, and evaluation of the work at hand. In the third year, assign tasks to specific organizations, hold one another accountable, and share leadership.

> **Congratulations, party dudes!**
>
> If your collaboration is able to embed changes into individual organizations—if you are able to reduce your need for a collaboration "coordinator"—then your group has achieved something remarkable. You've changed the system! Celebrate, celebrate, celebrate. (Disco music optional.)

In such ways, collaboration is embedded into the fabric of the community. Member agencies learn to work with each other so that collaborations last beyond any one individual's tenure. To cement this change, consider training board members or senior staff members in the partner organizations on communications, conflict management, and project planning as the topics relate to collaboration. This is the most sophisticated way of collaborating, and your board or staff may need an opportunity to do some structured thinking about it.

Action Step

If your collaboration does not require a permanent coordinator, begin now to plan a phase-out of that position. Begin planning today for the budget changes your organization will need to absorb the jobs the coordinator is doing.

Chapter Summary

This chapter has listed many ways nimble collaborations describe (and seek) the results they want to accomplish. All the energy devoted to a collaborative effort is wasted unless it focuses on specific results everyone wants to achieve; therefore, nimble collaborations make sure results are at the heart of each step they take. Results are first discovered as partners talk about the premise and promise of the collaboration. Next, results are written down as mission, vision, and outcome statements. Finally, the evaluation carefully measures success in terms of those results.

Collaboration is important because together organizations can achieve results they cannot achieve alone. The next chapter explores the ways that togetherness can help—or hinder—the achievement of results.

Chapter Two

Shape Relationships

Winston Churchill said, "First we shape our dwellings, then our dwellings shape us." Collaboration works in a similar way: First we shape our relationships; then our relationships shape our work. Much of the frustration that people endure in the beginning of a collaboration involves patiently defining relationships among members.

When your organization collaborates with another agency, you enter into a relationship with it. The more you both know about this relationship at the outset, the easier it is to nurture a collaboration that rewards all the members. Each partner agency works at developing the important competencies that sustain positive working relationships, including the competence to

- Build trust
- Reveal your self-interest
- Invite all organizations that can contribute
- Define core organizations
- Clarify roles
- Plan to communicate key information

Build Trust

Trust is the key indicator of the potential for success. Whether the collaboration is strengthening ties that already exist or building trust with a new partner organization, it needs to know the elements of trust building that are crucial to engaging in conflict and in changing complex systems.

To build trust, share hope. All participants must believe that the mission and vision of the collaboration is the right thing to do, and that the collaboration can achieve its goals to some degree. When agencies share hope, more energy is available to stay committed to the process.[8]

---

8 Thanks to Michael Winer of Synoptics, Boise, Idaho,
   for the idea.

Also remember that collaborations bog down when one or more partners "just want to do the work we need to do to satisfy the funder." Keep the collaboration's intended results public and spend time renewing commitment to them. (For more help, review Chapter One.)

Finally, acknowledge—again—that each organization will have to change. Collaboration is a process best used to change an ineffective system to a more effective system. Since each organization in the collaboration is part of the system, each has a part of the problem. Members of the collaboration should expect to influence each other to make necessary changes.

Exercises for building trust—brief activities in ongoing sessions—can be effective right away. If your organization is waiting to trust other members of the collaboration before committing to it, then you are doubling your work. Trust is like swimming: You can read about it, practice it on the beach, and make sure a qualified lifeguard is at hand. But eventually you will have to leap into the water. If your careful inspection of the tides doesn't turn up any jellyfish or shark fins, then you need to leap.

Trust happens as you work. Consultant and trainer John Scherer said it well: "You build trust by sharing data and clarifying expectations."[9] These tasks and others are addressed in the following pages.

Reveal Your Self-Interest

It's easy to assume that we know what each person and each organization wants out of a project or special effort. When self-interests mesh, we call it a "win-win" scenario; when self-interests seem to clash, partners can get secretive. When self-interest is not discussed openly, we tend to look for "hidden agendas" and guess what another person desires.

Healthy collaborations do not operate in this manner. Instead, organizations and people articulate what they want and need. Self-interest (whether the individual self or the organizational "self") is the prime mover of people and organizations. It shouldn't be judged as "good" or "bad"—it just is! When you talk about your organization's self-interest, you are exposing what used to be its hidden agenda. You legitimize concerns and create an atmosphere that invites discussion about important issues. One of the first dramatic changes that people observe in healthy collaborations is, "We have no secrets."

When partners help each other get what they need, they help the project move forward. Self-interest is a code word for *passion*. Once a person's passion is hooked, that person's commitment is hooked. To judge someone else's self-interest as good

---

[9] J. Scherer and J. Sherwood, "A Model for Couples: How Two Can Grow Together," *Journal of Small Group Behavior*, Vol. 6 No. 1 (February 1975).

A true fable . . . Self-interest in action

It was the end of the second year of the collaboration to reduce youth crime. The partners included the director of a mental health organization, the director of county social services, the local school superintendent, and the local police chief. The most recent meeting of the partners focused on evaluation, and the discussion pulsed with honest feedback from one agency to another. The police chief was especially adamant about the unmet needs and problems of kids he saw in crisis—good kids who were headed in the wrong direction. "Look," he said, "we've seen some of these kids again and again. They need a kind of help we're not equipped to give. We're corrections officers, not counselors—my people are not trained for this." He looked hard at the mental health provider, whose agency was known for its slow responses.

The meeting was almost over, and people were exhausted but reluctant to leave because they had been pretty hard on the mental health provider—and he'd been pretty quiet. In fact, he looked shell-shocked. Finally, he said, "What you want me to do is to respond within three hours for any crisis you report. I'd have to put my staff on beepers and set up a 24-hour schedule. You've got to be kidding!"

The director of county social services was kind and firm, "You can ramp up gradually, add some hours now, and go to 24 hours by the end of the year. We'll help you in any way we can. We need this service, and we want you to provide it." The mental health provider was reluctant. "My board won't go for this kind of change in service." But the school superintendent didn't let that excuse ride. "I know your board chair very well. I'll help you talk it out with her."

The partners knew that the mental health services were below par, and finally something was being done. The police chief smiled to himself; perhaps there'd be some real help for the most troubled kids in crisis he saw every day. His self-interest prevailed, and services to kids would be better for it.

or bad limits access to self-interest's enormous power to accomplish things. One way to stop judging self-interest is to try to find the "enlightened self-interest" that a person may be trying to express. Openly discussing self-interest can be so unsettling that it takes repeated attempts to get the issue clear. Still, this discussion is an important way to move your relationship with other organizations forward. This helps everyone understand what an organization needs to stay involved.

An example of revealing self-interest emerged during the mid-1980s for the partners of a small collaboration in a rural community in the Midwest:

> The partners hoped to create more effective medical care for migrant farm laborers who were currently using the local hospital emergency room for all their health needs. The collaboration included representatives from the migrants along with the hospital and public health and social services agencies. At their very first meeting, the facilitator went around the table and elicited statements of self-interest from all the participants. Everyone talked about "what's in it for me."

They all knew what the hospital wanted: reduced use of the emergency room. Treating nonemergency illnesses, like the flu, and providing prenatal care were expensive in an emergency room setting. The hospital wanted to save money and resources by establishing other ways for migrants to get routine health care. It was a relief to talk about this goal openly and respectfully as self-interest.

Many people were shocked when the director of social services said, "I'm not sure what my organization's self-interest is, but my personal self-interest is to get my boss's job." They relaxed as she explained that her boss was the county administrator, and he was retiring soon. "This collaboration is a great platform for me to show the county commissioners that I can be a great administrator," she said.

During the first year of the project, collaboration partners used self-interest to steer the way they implemented their tasks. For instance, they set up a careful tracking system to see if the hospital was actually saving money when other services were available for migrants to use. When the collaboration finally proved that it was saving the hospital money, the hospital entered into negotiations to put a small portion of those savings back into the collaboration.

And the director of social services? The partners all agreed to make sure she was visible to the county commissioners. She made all the reports to the county board, and, when a television station came to do a story about the collaboration, she was the "star." In return for this visibility, she worked hard to make sure that all the information going out to the public was correct, and that brochures, reports, and other documents were professional looking. At the end of the first year, the partners estimated that she had spent the equivalent of $6,000 in clerical support and document production. Instead of looking like a little, grant-funded, funky collaboration, the partners came off as an innovative and professional group. Because the collaboration looked and felt professional, it garnered the all-important support of the local doctors.

By the way, yes, she did get the administrator's job.

Action Step

When you are ready to describe your agency's interests and listen to the interests of other agencies and individuals, you are ready to enter into a win-win relationship with your peers. Put self-interest on the agenda for an upcoming collaboration meeting. Because interests change, put it on the agenda again in six months and see if agency interests are clearer or, perhaps, have changed.

A true fable . . . Bringing new faces to the collaboration table

A big city in the Midwest was experiencing the same problems a lot of big cities face: A neighborhood that used to be primarily industrial had gone to seed, most of the buildings abandoned. A big swath of unused rail lines cut through these blocks, providing a nice environment for rats and crime. The newly elected mayor had run on a promise to convert this area to a shiny new jewel for the city, and he promptly set up a planning task force that included all the usual players: the municipal development office manager, a representative from the state environmental office, a couple of big corporate-type developers, and representatives from community groups.

The task force spent eighteen months looking at options for redeveloping the area and finally hit upon a plan that seemed satisfactory to most folks: a mix of upscale town homes near an upscale marketplace of small shops, a handful of small office buildings or light-use manufacturing, and some affordable-housing apartment buildings. The whole neighborhood would be glued together by a kind of linear park created out of the space where the rail lines used to lie. The mayor was delighted when the city council approved the whole plan and asked the task force to become an implementation group—a committee responsible for putting the plan into action.

That's when the real trouble started. Instead of a positive response to the plan, the local newspaper threw stones at it, calling the apartment buildings a "disguise for affordable housing—don't working folks have a right to something better?" Then communities of color began to complain, as there were no representatives from them on the implementation committee. And just to give the mayor plenty of headaches, the environmental report was very negative; the city would probably have to get funds from the state's Office of Environmental Disasters for cleanup work before any building could begin.

The implementation committee felt picked on. For instance, some committee members groused privately that they had included communities of color in the surveys conducted during the planning phase. The corporate developers had donated months of time so that they could get in on the ground floor once building actually began. And now they were getting political pressure to include other groups in building and ownership opportunities. Furthermore, committee members wondered how they could get anything done if the committee doubled in size.

After a lot of dithering, committee members hired a consultant to help them build a collaborative approach to bringing in the right people. They spent two months thinking through what to do and how to do it. Eventually, they set up a subcommittee for affordable housing and a subcommittee for cultural competence. These subcommittees were given specific decision-making authority on broad parts of the development plan, and they each sent a representative to the main implementation committee. That committee also invited two representatives from nonprofit housing and community-building organizations to join discussions. A special half-day meeting brought everybody on board and made sure they were all welcomed as equals. And, finally, the corporate developers all signed a document limiting their ownership of the new housing that would be built. This opened the door for the nonprofit groups and smaller developers to get a piece of the pie also.

The implementation committee and the subcommittees were present months later when the first cornerstone of the first building was laid. The next day the newspaper had a two-page spread—all positive—about the "city's newest jewel of a neighborhood." By inviting new members in at the right time and organizing in the right fashion, the implementation committee had dramatically altered development plans, and had started on a project that excited everybody in town.

Invite All Organizations That Can Contribute

Meticulous assessment of membership is critical to collaboration success. Are the right organizations at the table? Trust and the efficacy of results will increase if each organization that has something to give to the system is part of the collaboration.

At this moment, your collaboration is probably successfully aligned with all the organizations that it finds easy to work with. Now is the time to add those organizations your collaboration is *unfamiliar* with. Invite these new partners to the table in ways that respect them and interest them. If your current partners are all agencies you know, then go back to the drawing board. Is the collaboration, in its current form, simply relying on a limited clique to do the work?

Collaboration becomes more nimble when every agency that is part of the problem or the solution is involved. All of these groups may not be present at each meeting; to be nimble is to engage the right people in the right activity at the right time. (More about that later.) But collaboration is a process for systems change, and it requires every element of that system to be represented in some way. The agency you avoid because it competed with you during the last funding cycle should be at the table. The agency you distrust because its political agenda is so different should be at the table. The agency you consider "too little" or "too big" must be at the table as well.

Look around your meeting table. Are the same old (and reliable) faces there? Who is missing? What agencies never send representatives? How can you invite them so that they understand their self-interest? Where are the communities of faith? Where are the service clubs? What are you doing to bring new faces and new resources into the meeting room? Nimble collaboration can lead you to discover community resources you never knew existed.

> ### Who are you working with?
>
> You automatically invite the organizations you trust and the people you like to work with you. However, collaboration is an opportunity to work with *every* organization that contributes to the system, including those organizations you don't trust or those people you find irksome. It's been said that *collaboration is the art of working with jerks,* and sometimes it seems that way. But those "jerks" can become surprisingly strong allies (though perhaps still irksome) when rallied around a common vision.

Some collaborations need to work on their cultural competence. "We invited people of color, but nobody came," partners complain. Most likely, this collaboration has not yet found the appropriate or productive way to invite minority members to the table. Ways to build diversity include

- Interview key leaders in the community. What is their advice on getting people's interest and time?

- Visit with parents and small business owners who are members of that community. What is important to them? What topics ignite their passion?

- Look for collaborations that are culturally competent. Ask them to train you.

- Think through the possible self-interests of various groups. Spell out what's in it for them to engage with you in this work. Some organizations may not have had the opportunity to consider "what's in it for us." Talk to them about their self-interest.

Action Step

A collaboration cannot be nimble if it is tripping over the organizations that are not part of the partnership. Discuss the current representation in your collaboration. Is every group that is part of the system—the solution or the problem—represented in some form? Don't rush out and invite folks, and don't assume that all these people need to be involved in every detail of the collaboration. Figure out what you need, and seek help from the community in finding new members.

Define Core Organizations

Getting the right people at the collaboration table talking about the right things is only part of the job. Once there, organizations need to be used intelligently. In an orchestra, the strings are placed in front and the percussion instruments move to the back of the hall, where they won't overwhelm the more delicate instruments. In a similar way, the partners in a collaboration must find their appropriate places.

In particular, you may want to name the core members of your collaboration: the agencies closest to the action that are expected to participate in most of the meetings and activities of the collaboration. Which organizations are central to achieving the mission? Which organizations are important but not essential? Which organizations need to be informed and involved but are not part of everyday business?

As you answer these questions, plot the organizations on a *membership ring*, which looks like a target that archers use. Figure 2: Membership Ring, on page 40, illustrates this structure.

The different rings on the target break out this way:

- The collaboration's desired results and the clients, consumers, or community residents for whom those results are designed are at the center—the bull's-eye. (Chapter One provides more information about how a nimble collaboration always keeps results "front and center.")
- Organizations that actually talk to the consumer, that work closely with the consumer, and that design and deliver services and products are in the first ring.
- The second ring is for resource and referral-type or marketing-type agencies that provide the consumer with information, or that refer the consumer to organizations in the first ring.

- In the third ring are groups that are involved with but not central to the consumer or the client. These organizations need to be kept informed because they can give good advice to the core partners.

Figure 2: Membership Ring

Participants in nimble collaborations ask the organizations in the first ring outside the bull's-eye to be central or "core" partners. *These organizations form the ring of shared leadership.* (In Chapter Three, you'll read more about how shared leadership helps a collaboration sustain itself.) Groups in the second ring are usually part of the collaboration, and their involvement may be keyed to specific tasks or roles. They may (or may not) be part of everyday decision making for the collaboration. Finally, the third ring is for member organizations that are communicated with regularly or asked to give input for a specific decision, but are not actively involved in the collaboration.[10]

The target structure is especially important for collaborations involved in improving service delivery for clients. We will revisit the structure briefly in Chapter Four: Collaborate to Integrate Services.

Action Step

Create target structure for your collaboration—one that involves the right organizations at the right time in the right activities.

---

[10] Thanks to Pam Curtis, policy advisor, Governor's Office of Health, Human Service and Labor, State of Oregon, for her target structure idea.

A true fable . . . Target restructure puts collaboration on track

County Commissioner Olsen's county consisted largely of residential suburbs of a major city. Soon after her election, she had become the head of the family service collaboration. She had gotten involved because she believed this collaboration could make a real difference for both healthy families and distressed families that needed deeper social supports. She thought of it as a place to tie schools, libraries, social services, and public health agencies into a single stream, an easily accessible product.

The collaboration, however, baffled Commissioner Olsen. It could not seem to build an integrated network of services. In particular, she couldn't get the schools to pay attention. The six school districts in the county only gave lip service to the collaboration. The school superintendents never attended meetings but instead sent people who didn't seem to fit the collaboration. This one, just now was moaning, "This is add-on work for me, you know, I go back to my real job when I leave this collaboration meeting." Obviously this principal didn't have a clue about the real work in front of the partners.

In her heart, though, Commissioner Olsen couldn't blame the principal. The meetings never had the agenda the principal wanted them to have. People at the table focused on minutiae and couldn't seem to break loose. As a matter of fact, the principal was the only participant at the meetings who was a senior leader in an organization.

Commissioner Olsen vowed then and there to reassess the structure of this service integration collaboration—to involve other leaders appropriately. After a few meetings with the collaboration coordinator and input from a consultant, she realized that the collaboration needed to have several teams working at the same time. The teams should include one for program managers to talk about the minutiae that was currently swamping the agenda for the whole collaboration; one for administrators to help them grasp how service integration was going to change their products and services; and one for the community's elected officials and senior leaders so that they would be ready to make the policy and funding changes needed to fully integrate services for families.

During the summer she approached the school superintendents. Wouldn't it make sense for them to meet with her and the school board chairs as a kind of education leadership council for the county? Some of the superintendents balked at asking the board chair to attend another meeting, but finally a first date was set.

The meeting went well, and Commissioner Olsen had an opportunity to explain how the collaboration was reorganizing itself. Nobody jumped up and down with glee, but they did all admit that talking to one another about countywide education and family issues could provide an important frame for the decisions they made for their own school districts. With the new structure in place, the collaboration began to get more results—and participants quit complaining, because their time was spent wisely.

Clarify Roles

The collaboration has a membership ring. Each member organization has its place in the structure, and each sends a person to the meetings. Now, what role will each person play in the collaboration?

Collaborations start on a person-to-person basis and move as quickly as possible beyond individual personalities. This movement calls for clarifying roles—a key to embedding collaborations into the fabric of the community so they do not depend on certain people. Sorting out roles is part of nurturing relationships that work.

Collaboration mystery revealed

Do not try to achieve "buy-in" from people or organizations by asking them to attend meetings. Construct a membership ring and ask core organizations to be core partners. Find other ways to engage the rest of the important agencies and people in your effort.

Most roles should be put in writing and agreed to by partners. Does your collaboration suffer because individuals sometimes don't do what they say they will do? This accountability issue may be based in role confusion. Make sure that every person who attends collaboration meetings has a job description, and that every person's agency signs off on the job description in writing.

Another important element in role clarification is to have people with similar roles working together at least part of the time. Senior leadership meets together, program or mid-management people meet together, and direct service or frontline staff meet together. While the nimble collaboration may not have these role-related people meet often, it's still important to have people with similar jobs exchange information and together make decisions that have systemwide impact.

Key roles include

- Initiator
- Convener and facilitator
- Special point of contact
- Agency representative
- Client
- Funder
- Fiscal agent and lead agency
- Consultant

Initiator

Many collaborations start because one or two people have a good idea, share it, and get excited about its potential. These people are *initiators:* They have a result in mind and they can attract people and other important resources to work toward that result.

Initiators have a key responsibility if they want to construct a nimble collaboration: They must build trust by being open and inclusive in their behaviors. In particular, this means that initiators must be able to accept revisions to their personal vision and include other people's ideas about what is important to do.

Initiators are good at starting things; often, they're not good at maintaining long and complex negotiations. The nimble collaboration allows initiators to move out of the leadership chair as the process draws out. The following case illustrates how one collaboration created a graceful exit for a fine and powerful initiator.

Commissioner Adams was a hero to the Family Life Collaboration that linked social services and recreation facilities. Family Life wanted vital new connections in programming, such as linking teen sports programs to efforts by the county public health department to eliminate sexually transmitted diseases. The collaboration needed the support of at least one county government leader, so it asked Commissioner Adams to be the initiator.

Commissioner Adams took this effort to heart and spent hours convincing his colleagues, county department executives, and the public that the Family Life Collaboration was a good idea. As usual, he played the role of initiator well, and other important people participated in the meetings because he was there—even if it was just to protect their turf from his busy hands! As discussions evolved, the commissioner began to incorporate other people's ideas into the plan, the mark of the gifted initiator. He succeeded in getting the county public health department to set aside a staff person to coordinate this new effort.

Unfortunately, as time went by, Commissioner Adams began participating less and less in the collaboration meetings. Partners there were getting down to the nitty-gritty details—policies to be revised, program schedules to be modified, and use of space to be changed. The commissioner even missed the meeting where budgets were altered.

Collaboration partners were accustomed to the commissioner's participation in the meetings and were unsure about whether or not to move forward without him. After a long discussion, they decided that Bob should talk to Commissioner Adams. Bob was the senior administrator of the county social services department and had a great working relationship with the commissioner.

Through Bob, the partners wanted to convey an invitation and a message to the commissioner. The invitation was to a countywide celebration of the Family Life Collaboration, at which they would honor Commissioner Adams for his support. The message was that his name was being removed from the roster of regular meetings. The partners were nervous about removing an elected official, but they needed to get on with their work without worrying about his participation.

Bob told Commissioner Adams that the work of initiator was successfully accomplished. What's more, the commissioner would be kept up-to-speed on the progress of the collaboration through the regular weekly update (distributed on e-mail) and through casual conversation with Bob. No, the commissioner did not need to put the regular collaboration meetings on his schedule anymore.

The commissioner was delighted. The celebration was well attended, and Commissioner Adams continued his support of the collaboration. Later that year he took some influential foundation board members to lunch where he showcased the results of the collaboration and pushed hard for further funding.

Convener and facilitator

Another important person during start-up is the *convener*. A convener is good at collecting the right people at the right time. Often a convener will rely on an initiator's ability to attract people to the work, and then will build on that success by continuing to involve more of the right people.

A convener may also be a good group *facilitator*. If not, then someone must be selected to facilitate the meetings of the potential partners in the collaboration. One of the most important ways to conquer meeting ennui during this first stage is to make sure meetings are effective—focused on results and role clarity. A good facilitator can do that.

Special point of contact

A partner with good communication skills can play the *special point of contact* (SPOC) role.[11] The SPOC directs mail, phone calls, and e-mail to the people best able to respond. The SPOC is a "human switchboard," routing calls and communiqués from the outside to the right partner and keeping the collaboration members in touch with each other. A SPOC can help people decide when a special or extraordinary meeting is needed to respond nimbly to some emerging circumstance or conflict.

The SPOC provides both a public voice for the collaboration and a "private line" that connects partners. This role is especially useful if the collaboration is having difficulty bringing conflicts into the open. Collaborations that have a collaboration coordinator may include this role as one of the coordinator's duties. Some collaborations discover that once the role of SPOC is taken care of, the job description for the coordinator changes considerably.

Agency representative

Most participants are at the collaboration to represent their agencies. *Agency representatives* wear two hats: They must represent the work of the collaboration at the home agency, and they must represent the work of the home office at the collaboration. Agency representatives have a responsibility to act in ways that build trust in themselves and their agencies. How is that done?

---

[11] Bone Hicks, *Self-Managing Teams* (Los Altos, CA: Crisp Publications, 1999).

A true fable . . . For want of a champion

In a large metropolitan community, professionals from many different youth agencies were meeting to find ways to pool nonallocated dollars. If they could just get a commitment from every agency's budget, they would have an interagency fund that could be spent on items that no "official" fund would pay for—cab fare to a therapist, athletic equipment, summer camp tuition, or any other unusual activity that might help a young person.

For months they discussed how to set up this fund and how much each agency should commit. For months Phil, the representative from corrections, had been avoiding telling his boss, Kathy, about this fund, although he himself was an enthusiastic supporter of it. Everyone at the table liked Phil; he was experienced, compassionate, and funny! Every month at the collaborative meetings he would say, "It's not time to talk to Kathy yet. She's not in the right place to support this yet." And every month the partners believed him because he was a seasoned corrections administrator and knew how to be political.

The day of reckoning arrived after eighteen months of work. Everyone at the collaboration meeting table came with a commitment from their organizations to the interagency fund, some for a few dollars and some for a lot. It was expected that corrections (a large agency and a potential big winner for this nonallocated fund) would commit $7,500. Phil had told his boss about this budget expenditure the day before. She came to the meeting with him, surprised and incensed. "How can you expect us to commit this kind of money?" she asked the partners angrily. "We must do what the judges tell us to do. We have to keep reserves in our budget for what the judges want. We can't make this commitment." After the meeting, she called several other senior administrators in other agencies. By the end of the week, eighteen months of work had collapsed.

Phil's failure to champion the collaboration—and his partners' failures to challenge him about that during all their meetings—nearly ended the collaboration.

First, representatives must be clear about the way their organizations are affected by the mission of the collaboration. Skillful members come to the collaboration meetings steeped in their agencies' self-interest. This can only happen if the representative is clear about what the home office wants from the collaboration.

Second, agency representatives must be clear about the nature of their role back at the office: They are *champions* for the work of the collaboration. They should be clear about whether they can make decisions for their home organizations or whether they need to go through layers. Nimble collaboration requires that agency representatives find ways to get quicker decisions from higher-ups on certain key issues. Colleagues at the collaboration table can share tips on how to speed decisions at the home office and should be frank with each other when they are having problems championing the collaboration at home. Following are some of the classic problems that occur at the home office and that alert agency representatives should address.

This they can do either by dealing with the problem directly at the home office or, when necessary, by bringing the problem to the collaborative partners for advice and assistance.

- Frontline staff who perceive any change in programming or activities as some sort of personal loss.

- Practitioners who evaluate collaboration *processes* rather than *outcomes* for customers. (For the distinction, see Chapter One.)

- Administrators who allow their agencies to run dual systems: the "regular" programs or operations and the collaboration "project" programs or operations.

- Managers who fail to draw the attention of the boss and other organization leaders to the collaboration's discoveries about best practices and improved services.

- Leaders who fail to budget for (or support) internal, agencywide adoption of the best practices or improved services the collaboration creates.

- Funders who move too quickly to the new, sexy innovation rather than help institutions incorporate and sustain best practices and changed programs over time.

Every agency representative has a duty to champion the collaboration inside his or her organization. This means transmitting the vision, values, and vitality of the collaboration to subordinates, peers, and superiors. It might be said that only 20 percent of the collaboration's work gets done around the table; 80 percent of the work of collaboration happens when individuals champion it back in their own offices. This hard work happens behind closed doors, where an organization struggles with the input and ideas generated by the collaboration and the response it demands of the agency. If a member can't champion those decisions, then another representative should be sent to the table.

Client

Nearly every systems change effort funded by state or federal government demands that the collaboration include clients, customers, or consumers in its planning activities—people whose bosses don't pay them to come to meetings.

There are many ways to involve customers. One is to create an alliance with an existing consumer advocacy group or advisory panel. For example, community education departments in schools have citizen advisory groups, and Head Start programs maintain parent advisory panels. Many nonprofits have organized customer service groups to get feedback from their customers or the people in their programs. Look for an existing group that can review the collaboration's plans for systems change and explain how that change will impact the consumer.

Involve consumers *only* in those portions of the meetings where the actual product or service delivery is discussed. For example, many systems change efforts focus on the complex relationships among bureaucracies. Sorting out these complexities is different from sorting out direct service delivery, and agency staff should settle their conflicts with each other privately, not in front of the consumer.

Be mindful and purposeful about adding consumers. Just inviting them to the table isn't good enough. Write up a consumer's role as a list of "expectations," and help consumers to create a list of expectations they have of you. Keep their involvement by having focused agendas and crisp meetings. Also consider finding a mentor or partner who will work with consumers and help them actively participate in the proceedings.

The most effective way to involve consumers is by getting their feedback on the product or the service as it is delivered and altering that product or service to address shortcomings. Think like a retailer! When customers don't like products, they don't buy them. What part of the collaboration's service dissatisfies customers? What are their most common complaints? Use an inexpensive paper-and-pencil evaluation form if the project is strapped for cash, or purchase one of the excellent consumer feedback systems that retailers use. Spend grant money on translators to help non-English speakers answer questions or on analysis to explain what the data mean. When there is a clear negative response by a statistically significant group of consumers, fix the problem!

Funder

One of the most prominent complaints about collaborations is that they get three to five years of support—and then the funder wants to do something new, something even more innovative. End of funding.

How do you keep funding support? By meeting the self-interests of funders, and by treating them as *equal* partners, no more and no less. They are one of the resources at your collaboration table, just as big agencies are resources for bureaucratic power and direct service delivery agencies are resources for consumers.

This doesn't mean that funders come to every meeting. It does mean that they know key information and that the collaboration has groomed their commitment, lit up their passion, and responded to their self-interest. If the collaboration members are not sure what their funder's commitment, passion, or self-interest is, then that's the first thing to discover. Is the private foundation mostly a "check writer," not interested in full participation as a full partner? Then how will you find out about and meet the foundation's interests? Is the collaboration funder a government group, like the state legislature? Then what key elected official needs to be informed about or involved with the collaboration in order for the legislature to stay passionate about the topic? Nimble collaborations don't just look for the fastest answer; they look for the answer with the biggest payoff.

In addition, you and your collaboration partners must find creative ways to communicate with funders about the successes and challenges of the collaboration. Many funders are experimenting, looking for best practices. They want to know what works and what doesn't, so feel free to tell them! Newsletters and reports may get only cursory readings. Spend time hatching more creative ways to keep funders informed. Assign one of the organizations in the collaboration to focus on this work. And ask other funders for help understanding the donor's perspective.

A collaboration may be tempted to ascribe more power to state and federal funders than they actually have. People from many state and federal programs promote collaboration without really knowing what it is. Talk to them, teach them, and stay in contact. Share your war stories and your success stories. Begin on day one, helping your funding partners understand their role in successfully altering the system.

Involving clients effectively

You can involve clients directly in the collaboration or seek their feedback. Here is an example of each approach.

Direct involvement. A government housing agency managed a campus of twenty-eight town homes in a mid-size town. Families in transition from homelessness, new immigrants, and job seekers rented these town homes. Many of the community members spoke English as a second language. Through a collaboration, the agency added tenants as representative members on the site management team. First the agency interviewed leaders in the tenant community, seeking names for appropriate people to serve as representatives. Then it contacted the volunteer coordinator from a large church nearby, seeking volunteers to mentor the new representatives. These volunteers attended meetings with a tenant representative, helping the representative understand the English proceedings and add to discussions during the meeting. Often, volunteer and representative would meet before the meeting to look over the agenda and get prepared.

Several friendships flowered among the volunteers and the representatives, and this often aided in the representative's family's transition—a key indicator that the collaboration was working for the tenants.

Involvement through feedback. In a small community in the Midwest, the senior meals program feeds approximately one hundred older adults one meal a day. A collaboration sprouted with a local health consortium to spread the word to these people about their risk for breast and colon cancer. Collaboration members had difficulty getting older people to use the health service, so they began asking the volunteers who delivered the meals to ask the clients some questions about those services. The feedback from the older adults was remarkable: Clinic hours were inappropriate, there was too long a wait for mammography, and some brochures led seniors to believe there was a fee for the service. The collaboration partners corrected these problems. Service use rate went up by 40 percent within the year!

Fiscal agent and lead agency

The *fiscal agent* is the organization that receives from the funder the money to operate the collaboration. The fiscal agent is responsible for seeing that the funds are spent legally. Depending on the organization's other involvement in the system, it may be an active partner, or it may simply hold and discharge funds, usually for a small fee.

Sometimes when funders or government agencies push for collaboration, they call for the creation of a *lead agency*. Often, the lead agency is simply the term they use for *fiscal agent*. Other times, the funder is looking for an agency to be the special point of contact—the contact between collaboration and funder. Unfortunately, the term *lead agency* implies leadership, power, and authority, and the designated "lead" agency may find other partners looking to it for all kinds of authority it does not (and should not) have.

Be sure of what the funder—and your collaboration—means by lead agency. Does the funder want a fiscal agent, an organization that is the primary point of contact between the funder and the collaboration, or something much bigger? Don't invest power or leadership expectations in the so-called lead agency beyond the power or leadership that particular agency needs to do its job for the collaboration.

> ### Tap into leadership from elected officials
>
> Elected officials across the nation have two essential pledges they must uphold: to be good stewards of resources, and to improve the lives of the citizens in their communities. These primary responsibilities can be one route to embedding improvements into the system. If your collaboration is successfully improving services and products for citizens, then the elected officials should build on your success by shifting existing resources to doing daily business in the new ways you've discovered.

In the nimble collaboration, different partners step up to the leadership role as they are needed. Leadership is a duty to be assumed within the collaboration, not assigned by an outside agent.

Consultant

From time to time, collaborations need to call in consultants, either for specific technical support, such as marketing or legal advice, or for more general organization development assistance. Consultants have a specific role that depends on the needs of the collaboration. They may offer *expertise*, serve as an *extra pair of hands*, or facilitate *process*.

Expertise: Marketers, accountants, and lawyers are all expertise consultants. So are knowledge experts, like the artist-in-residence who can help the art collaboration get involved in the community, or the lobbyist who can help the collaboration get laws passed. Many professions refer to these consultants as "technical assistants" because of their specialized knowledge or skill.

The role of the expert consultant is to provide a product for the collaboration. Often, partners treat this product as a "take-it-or-leave-it" product, such as a legal opinion or an audit. If a collaboration hires an expert consultant, it is important for the collaboration to define the product it wants as clearly as possible.

Extra Pair of Hands:[12] Many collaborations need help with tasks and goals that require broader knowledge or closer working relationships than a technical consultant can provide. For instance, collaborations may need to create and carry out fund development plans, or evaluate the collaboration's successes, or write procedural documentation. The pair-of-hands consultant plays a role more closely resembling that of a manager on the payroll of the collaboration or one of its members.

The role of the pair-of-hands consultant is to do work that wouldn't get accomplished otherwise. This can be a big help to the collaboration, especially if the consultant is well acquainted with the effort, such as a recently retired staff person from a partner organization. In this case, the collaboration must be clear about who supervises the consultant, what decisions he or she can make, and how the collaboration and the consultant will know if the consultant has done good work.

Process: This consultant is often used to facilitate meetings so that all the partners can participate fully. He or she may function as a "big-picture" thinker, helping the collaboration see the forest for the trees. In the last few years, some process consultants have become well acquainted with the collaborative way of doing business, and they can help partners learn how to manage the process of collaborating on their own.

The role of the process consultant is to help solve problems in the dynamics of the collaboration. This help is often sought when the collaboration encounters an apparently unsolvable problem. In this situation the consultant's role is to gather data, analyze the situation, and recommend steps to take. In addition, the consultant might perform specific duties, such as conflict management or meeting facilitation. Here again it is important for the collaboration to identify the problem as best it can before hiring the consultant (even if the problem is "help us identify our problem"), and to set out clear evaluation criteria so that everyone can know why the consultant is doing certain work and whether or not the consultant is doing good work.

Action Steps

Assign roles. Name roles for each partner in the collaboration, and then expect them to change over time. Consider writing "job descriptions" for each person who attends collaboration meetings, with the understanding that roles and jobs may change to keep things nimble. Layer meetings to help people with similar roles work together. For instance, a collaboration might split work up among the group of core partners, the direct service or frontline staff group, the mid-management group, and the senior leaders group. To be nimble might mean tossing the right decision to the right small group to make.

---

[12] Peter Block, *Flawless Consulting* (San Diego: Pfeiffer, 1981).

Discuss progress at the home office. As a standing item on meeting agendas, have members talk about what they've been saying about the collaboration back in their offices. How are they championing the work of the collaboration? Have they discussed with their home offices the duties of transmitting the vision, values, and vitality of the collaboration throughout the home agency? Do they need help convincing the boss or board that this work is valuable? Are they keeping staff up-to-date?

Find effective ways to involve end users. Nimble collaborations involve customers and consumers only in those meetings that are of interest to them. See the sidebar Involving Clients Effectively, page 48, for tips.

Find effective ways to involve funders. Assign one member the responsibility for developing a personal relationship with an appropriate program officer or government agency director. Use this relationship to keep the funders apprised of the collaboration's progress. Involve funders who are playing a more active role in the appropriate ring of the target structure.

Plan to Communicate Key Information

Communicating with all the members of a collaboration can be most frustrating. "They tease me about deforesting the countryside with all the paper I send them," one collaboration coordinator complained, "but somebody is always griping that they didn't get a notice, see a report, or know about *something*."

Communication that works well is communication that's planned well. When you consider the amount of work your collaboration is trying to complete, you see the picture: Not everyone needs the same information delivered in the same way. Instead of trying to say everything, just say what is most important in ways that people can hear it.

Accountable communications

Some people use knowledge as power. They'll say they didn't see a report about a decision so that they can make the group go back and revisit the decision. Be clear in the beginning who will get what written information and when they will get it. *Then hold people accountable to seek that information if they don't receive it automatically as planned.*

This means communicating differently with different agencies, an important way to "nimble-fy" your collaboration. The agencies in the first ring of the collaboration may need to be in direct and constant communication with one another. But collaboration members further from the center of action may have different communication needs.

Design a communications system that's sensitive to agency placement in the membership ring. Create a communications plan responsive to the different kinds of agencies and people in your collaboration. Talk to your partners about what information is most important to them and how they want to receive it. Balance these needs with the time and expense it will take to fulfill them.

As you strive for this balance, consider these options:

- Keep reports short. Focus on decisions and actions, not discussions.

- List decisions and actions as bulleted points under each result the collaboration wants to achieve. This is often a one- or two-page summary faxed weekly to core partners.

- Create a private e-mail link or newsgroup for core partners to relay everyday details of the work.

- Hold yourself accountable. If the same person always sends out meeting minutes and you don't get yours, ask for a copy. Don't blame the person for missing you!

- Be sure to include a place for kudos and good news in every piece you publish.

Collaboration mystery revealed

The following belief is false: "If we send everybody the same information, we'll keep each person's buy-in. Everybody will know everything!"

Everybody can't know everything. If the partners all clamor to know exactly what everybody said to everybody else as soon as it's said, then your collaboration has a trust issue. Work on trust, not on more new e-mails or newsletters.

Remember that people in the same membership ring can probably get the same kinds of communications. When you get to the last ring, usually the community at large, consider the reason you want to communicate with these people and organizations. Is it for referrals? Funding? Public relations? Public relations and marketing communications differ from member communications. By the time you reach the outer ring, bulletins or newsletters may be best. Ask your special point of contact (SPOC) to consider being the media link, nurturing relationships with local newspapers and radio and television stations.

Keep in mind the first law of communicating during change: People want more information than can possibly be provided. So make an agreement about what to communicate, in which format.

Action Step

Design a communications system that's sensitive to agency placement in the membership ring. Don't try to communicate all the information all the time to all the people—it's too complicated.

Chapter Summary

Relationships are built like a bridge, brick by brick, span by span. Nimble collaborations accept the paradox that you build trust by trusting. Some of the ways organizations go about trusting include revealing and serving self-interest, making sure all the right organizations are invited to join, defining and publishing the roles for those organizations and the people they send to represent them, and communicating the right information to the right groups.

"Turf issues" and "hidden agendas" are often cited as reasons collaborations fail. If partners focus on the results they want, and take active steps to groom productive relationships, then there are no such things as turf issues and hidden agendas. Instead, everyone's self-interests are legitimized, put on the table for discussion. And conflicts become the source of honest dialogue among partners in relationship with one another.

Thus, the nimble collaboration is developed, which can then turn its attention to sustaining itself. In Chapter Three we look for ways to be resilient, to keep on doing the work together that's so important to our agencies and our constituents.

Chapter Three

Structure for Resilience

Nimble collaborations are *resilient*—the third of the three key strategies for success. According to the *American Heritage Dictionary*, the word *resilience* means "elastic, capable of returning to original shape after being bent or stretched . . . recovering quickly." That definition offers an apt insight. Resilience implies the ability to stretch and bend, to undergo difficulties and yet return to a recognizable shape. A nimble collaboration is built elastically on a firm foundation so that it can deal proactively with the changing environment.

Collaboration is intricate work that occurs in the middle of a rapidly changing set of mandates, citizen interests, and funding. It's easy to get bogged down, especially if you are trying to change a system deeply steeped in bureaucracies. You need a platform that supports proactive thinking in dynamic circumstances and quick decision making that keeps the partners involved. You must first shape the structure, just as a skilled shipbuilder creates a sound hull. Structure is a sure indicator whether a collaboration will be nimble or crippled.

In this chapter you'll explore specific options for structuring your collaboration:

- Consider ten principles of resilience
- Refine your process for making decisions
- Share financial information
- Create a nimble governance system

In all these areas, you can build resilience. You can ensure that your collaboration survives the fantasies of policy makers, the vagaries of funders, and the inconsistencies of collaboration partners.

Consider Ten Principles of Resilience

A great way to make the collaboration nimble is to discuss the ten principles listed below. (Some of these have already been explained in previous chapters; for the sake of completeness they are echoed here.)

1. *The leadership of each participating agency energetically supports the results the collaboration aims to achieve.*

   Leaders and board members are keenly interested in results and want to know how the work is progressing. An annual report from the collaboration is not enough. The leaders of each partner agency understand and buy into the mission, values, and intended results of the collaboration.

2. *There is equity—not equality—of organizational power in the collaboration.*[13]

   Each organization that has something to contribute to the issue has a role in the collaboration. Some organizations have a bigger role or more influence than other partners, but there is space for each player in the game. Partners treat each other with respect, impartiality, and fairness.

   This principle recognizes that not every organization is the same; not every partner is an equal. Some partners are closer to the collaboration's central effort, and some make contributions and take rewards from a more distant position. The collaboration's work is planned to account for these differences.

3. *Systems are changed when individual organizations change themselves internally.*

   Wise collaborators strive for permanent systems change by demanding that parts of a system change. Each partner organization modifies its own policies, procedures, protocols, and priorities in the context of other agencies in order to create the best system for consumers. Collaboration leads to mutual institutional renewal.

4. *Leadership is shared among organizations.*

   There is no one leader in a collaboration, no single "big boss." All the partners are held accountable for results. Leadership may shift from agency to agency in a planned manner as the work progresses, and leaders are accountable for changing and renewing their own agencies in the context of the whole system. No agency in the collaboration is "better" or "more deserving" than any other, and each agency has a special contribution to make to the effort. Collaboration is the ultimate democracy.

5. *Conflict is expected and is managed effectively.*

   A key function of governance is to manage conflict. Strategies for resolving conflict are spelled out, and there is a clear list of who makes what decisions.

---

[13] See Winer and Ray, *Collaboration Handbook,* for more information on equity of power. Thanks to Michael Winer for the lexicon.

6. *Collaboration is transparent and does not create a new level of bureaucracy.*

   The collaboration does not constitute another hoop for local organizations to jump through in order to get funding. Likewise, collaborations do not create another door consumers must pass through in order to get service or product. A collaboration is not a new agency; it doesn't need a letterhead, an address, or a name. A collaboration doesn't hire staff, although it may support a temporary function called "coordinator" until the collaboration partners define how existing organizations will absorb functions that are necessary to sustain the collaboration.

7. *Each agency in a collaboration is accountable to its own leadership and its own constituents.*

   Though a collaboration exerts influence, it has no power to force an agency to do something. Funders are not the final authority; they are simply equal partners, no more and no less.

   Collaboration provides individual agencies with the opportunity to create policies for themselves that make sense in light of the bigger picture. Collaboration prompts and undergirds these institutional changes, with executives or board members finalizing changes their agencies make to achieve the goals of the collaboration.

   In collaborations with public sector organizations, elected officials are ultimately responsible for changes to public institutions. Nimble collaborations keep elected officials informed about the collaboration's progress. As potential changes to the public institutions are set out, the collaboration goes to the county board, school board, city council, or other body to gain approval for the changes.

8. *Decision making becomes faster and more effective as power to make decisions is delegated to appropriate subgroups.*

   Consumers and constituents should be in charge of the services and goods they buy or the things that happen to them. Good decisions are made as close to the consumer as possible. This may mean, for instance, that staff members who deliver direct services get involved in decision making in ways that are new to an agency.

   Decision-making structures and processes are closely tied to trust. The more partners trust one another, the easier it is to delegate decision making.

9. *Collaborations are usually impermanent.*

   Partners come together to achieve results they cannot achieve alone. Successful collaborations accomplish something; they change the system, refurbish organizations, generate new products or new resources, or involve citizens in new ways. The permanence of the change is assured when individual organizations of the collaboration prove that they have changed internally to accommodate better ways of doing business.

There are two exceptions to this principle: A collaboration becomes permanent when law demands it, or when the issue the collaboration addresses is so complex that a generation of work will be needed to make the change. (An example of such a collaboration can be found in Chapter Five.)

10. *Documentation supports resilience.*

    Written agreements spell out the vision, mission, and strategies of the collaboration. These agreements can be refined and rewritten as the work matures. Individual agencies change internal documents—such as standard operating procedures, job descriptions, and budgets—to reflect the new ways of getting things done.

Action Step

Share the ten principles of resilience with the senior managers and boards of all partner agencies in the collaboration. Promote nimbleness through discussions of these principles, so that leaders can see how collaborating is a unique way of doing business.

Refine Your Process for Making Decisions

In a nimble collaboration, decision making needs to be timely, with input from the right people and prompt responses to quick shifts in the environment. This section reviews key points about creating a decision-making structure that works for you, your partners, and your stakeholders.

There are three basic structures for making decisions:

- Autocratic—one person or a small group makes the decision
- Democratic—everyone has a vote and everyone votes on everything
- Diffuse—small groups make decisions assigned to them

More details about each structure follow.

Autocratic decision making

Autocratic decisions occur when just a few people decide what to do. Autocratic decisions are useful during a crisis or to get a group "off the dime" and moving. Your collaboration was probably begun autocratically if a small group of people wrote a grant for the effort or called the first meeting.

Collaborations may be initiated through autocratic action, but autocratic and collaborative styles do not often mesh. Collaborations usually quickly enter into a democratic decision-making process.

Democratic decision making

The majority wins—that's democratic decision making, and it should begin early in a collaboration. As mentioned earlier, most collaborations begin with every organization being represented at the table: one seat and one vote for every agency. This is the natural way to convene the partners and develop the vision and purpose of the collaboration.

Figure 3: Democratic Decision Making, below, illustrates this structure. Everyone sits around the meeting table, and each organization has a vote on each decision. Who runs this collaboration? All the partners do, by voting on all decisions.

Figure 3: Democratic Decision Making

Core Partner Table

Democratic decision making offers key benefits early on in a collaboration. For one, this structure is a great way to build trust and personal commitment to a collaboration. Some collaborations strive for consensus during this period (everyone agrees; the vote is unanimous), preferring to keep discussion alive until everyone thinks the proposed solution is the most workable.

Democratic decision making can also develop cohesion in the group. If you and your partners are struggling with trust issues, begin by making small democratic decisions together: where to meet, whether or not to have a facilitator. Making all of these early choices in a democratic way can build trust. In the process, you share data, clarify expectations, and build a culture for individual trust (even when individual members of the collaboration do not trust one another's organizations).

Democratic decision making is useful for building trust at start-up, for gradually restoring shattered trust, for ensuring buy-in and support for major policies, and for making critical decisions that affect the direction of the collaboration. But democratic processes can be decidedly un-nimble.

i

Democratic processes can be decidedly un-nimble.

Diffuse decision making

As a collaboration succeeds and grows, democratic decisions become cumbersome. Decisions depend on lengthy, time-consuming, and expensive group discussions. Nimble collaborations learn to delegate some decision making to small groups—to use diffuse decision making.

Figure 4: Diffuse Decision Making, below, illustrates this advanced, nimble collaboration structure. Here many work teams operate fairly independently on different tasks. Agencies and people who are not part of the regular membership work as equals.

Figure 4: Diffuse Decision Making

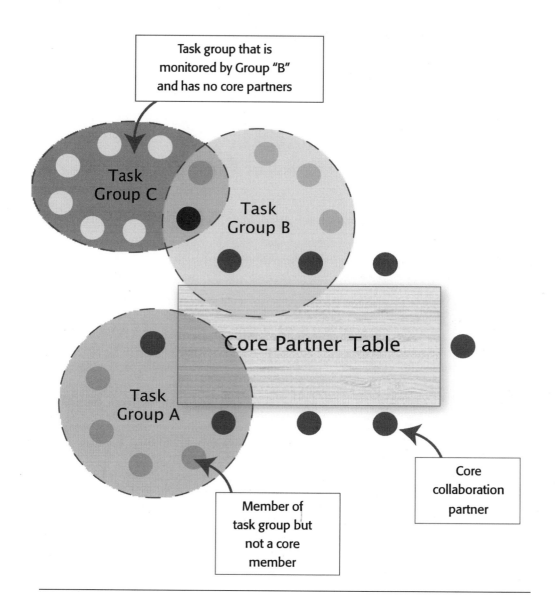

A true fable . . . Diffuse decision making at work

A collaboration of three rural electric cooperatives in the South had a decision to make. They knew the results they wanted to create would require shared information technology, especially communications software. They could ask two of the cooperatives to adopt the third's system, or they could purchase a new system altogether. The core partners of this collaboration struggled with this decision. It kept coming up on the agenda meeting after meeting.

Finally, the partners admitted their ignorance about the technical aspects of the decision and delegated it to the three cooperatives' computer specialists as a special task force. These computer specialists added the local computer store proprietor to the task force. They got clear instructions from the core partners in the collaboration:

"This is a level 2 activity, so bring us your best recommendation. We'll know your recommendation is good if:

• "You can train all users on the new software in the next eight months.

• "The system allows all users to access the communications software with a few keystrokes.

• "The system will support the engineers in the planned upgrade of data collection, such as peak hours of consumer use.

• "It meets all county, state, and federal guidelines.

• "It costs less than $125,000 from purchase to implementation."

The special task force did the research and prepared a specific option for the collaboration. Meanwhile, the regular meetings of partners focused on all the other important work at hand instead of grappling (ignorantly!) with this highly technical decision. The specialists brought in their recommendation, and the core partners of the collaboration reviewed it. They then directed their agencies to implement the decision.

Who runs this collaboration? The collaboration is run by the core members, whose organizations are central to the work and who chair the committees and task forces. (You identified core members when you plotted names on the membership ring described in Chapter Two; see page 39-40.) Core members set the mission, strategies, and results. They continue to meet to move the process along, and they assign tasks to subgroups.

This structure still provides interaction for all the members at periodic (often monthly) meetings. Yet the structure releases the energy and creativity of the group by empowering smaller, more agile teams to do certain tasks.

A diffuse structure also allows "outsiders" to impact the collaboration's work and increase creativity. It allows people and agencies that are not part of the regular collaboration to become involved in subcommittees or task forces. Many organizations may want to be part of the collaboration's work or influence the decisions it makes, but they are unable to be part of the whole collaboration. A diffuse structure gives them a place to be heard and to contribute.

A diffuse structure depends on the best possible processes for delegating tasks and decision making. Delegating is not saying to a person or team, "You decide." Instead, this structure assigns a level of responsibility to the person or team. Then it tells them how to know when they've made a good decision. For instance:

Level 1—Gather information, make a decision, and implement it. Tell the core partners what you did.

Level 2—Gather information and recommend a specific option.

Level 3—Gather information, list options, and bring all those options back to the core partners.

As an example, consider that grantwriting is often done in two stages. The first stage is keeping an eye out for good grant opportunities for the collaboration. Some collaborations assign this to the coordinator as an ongoing level 2 responsibility. The second stage is developing a specific grant and writing the application. Some collaborations assign a level 1 responsibility to their grantwriter, asking only to approve the final draft.

Carefully describe what a successful decision will look like, and tell people what they cannot do. Then delegation of decisions will not become a crapshoot. Put your protocol for making decisions in writing. Then, ask core members to sign off on it;

A sample decision-making protocol

We agree to abide by this decision-making process:

1. We talk about issues at this table, maintaining confidentiality until a decision is reached.

2. We share all relevant data freely, collecting information that helps us make decisions.

3. We set out to achieve consensus. We do not take "positions" early in our discussions. If a particular agency says no to a particular decision, then that agency clearly and honestly states why. All partners help to solve problems, create alternative solutions, or act in other ways to help that agency perceive alternatives to saying no.

4. If we cannot agree after two or three meetings, we set aside special meeting time with a facilitator to focus on this decision. If we still cannot come to consensus, then we call a moratorium on this issue and take it up again at a specified time.

5. We identify exactly what type of decisions will be made by the coordinator of the collaboration, by the executive committee of the collaboration, and by the full group of core members of the collaboration. We respect these boundaries.

6. We represent the consensus decisions of this group in a positive light to our individual boards. We live with our individual boards' decisions.

7. We remember that we cannot dictate what an agency should do or could do, and that the changes we need to make are the changes our community wants us to make. We're operating in a big picture, and we are accountable to all the families in our community, not just to each other.

simply including the protocol in meeting minutes isn't good enough, because how decisions get made is often at the heart of conflicts among partners. Get your collaboration members to pay more attention to the decision-making processes you want to use.

When writing policies for diffuse decision making in your collaboration, you may benefit by adapting John Carver's work on effective boards.[14] He suggests these principles:

- *Formulate broad policies first.* The partners in a collaboration should establish control over large issues and then decide how much further detail to go into. This approach avoids two mistakes. One is trying to micromanage program staff at the home office or teams within the collaboration. The other is allowing various teams to develop policies, which are then simply rubber-stamped by the collaboration as a whole.

- *Focus on who will benefit and at what cost.* This means turning attention away from personnel issues, programs, or finances and refocusing on why the collaboration exists—the collaboration's vision for the community.

- *Control delegated tasks by limiting, not prescribing.* Prescriptive policies restrict creativity and nimbleness. Instead, the core members in a nimble collaboration should set up "fences"—policies that mark what is unacceptable or "out of bounds." Within these limits, staff members act creatively and nimbly to implement policies. Core members do not get mired in details about the means to the ends.

In short, nimble collaborations do not burden themselves with lengthy lists of rules or bylaws. They write up a few broad policies, which they may include in a letter of agreement. One collaboration has just these:

1. "Don't do anything illegal.
2. "Don't spend more money than is allocated to the task or the result we want.
3. "Use consensus-driven decision-making processes.
4. "Excellent customer service—as perceived by the customer—is preeminent.*"

Action Step

Review your collaboration's existing policies. Are they prescriptive, or do they provide appropriate limits while encouraging diffuse decision making? Have you decided which decisions are level 1, level 2, and level 3? Carefully describe what a successful decision will look like, and tell people what they cannot do. Put your protocol for making decisions in writing and ask core members to sign off on it. A nimble collaboration puts time into this groundwork so that everyone feels decisions are made fairly. This platform also makes quick decisions easier.

---

[14] Material adapted from several works by John Carver, a consultant, an author, and the principal in Carver Governance Design, Inc., which works with nonprofit organizations on governance and the board-executive partnership.

Share Financial Information

Good ideas live and die by the dollar. Your responsibility to your collaboration partners in fiscal matters revolves around planning and changing the way parts of the system spend resources. Funding and budgets are often the source of unspoken tension at the collaboration table. When you discuss financial matters openly, you respect your relationship with one another, and you can look for solutions to long-term financial stressors.

If your collaboration is operating from a grant award, remember that you won't get grant money forever. Funders expect you to integrate what you discover into your organizations' regular budgets and standing financial plans. This expectation aligns with a principle of nimble collaboration—systems are changed when individual organizations change themselves internally. Since budgets and finance express an organization's structure, finance practices need to change to express the internal organizational changes. Discussing finances can be risky, though. Here are natural steps to take to reduce the fear when sharing financial information.

Expose detailed financial information

One of the most valuable ways to build trust is to call a meeting exclusively for executives of the collaboration agencies and have them expose specific financial information about specific programs, focusing on one program at a time. To facilitate this discussion, ask the executives to bring a document organized in three columns as follows:

- Column 1 lists all the services and products offered by the organization that are associated with the specific program under discussion.
- Column 2 shows how much money the agency spends on each service or product, and where the money comes from.
- Column 3 identifies how much it costs per client or per unit of service to run the program.

Figure 5: Sharing Financial Information, on pages 65 and 66, provides a sample of what this chart looks like. For illustration purposes, only two organizations are shown. In practice, all partners providing services should share their data in a similar format.

County Public Health Department and the nonprofit organization Clinica de la Familia are two members of a collaboration to improve the health of new babies. Following are charts showing financial information for these two organizations.

FIGURE 5: Sharing Financial Information

Clinica de la Familia Migrant Health Care and New Mom Follow-up

Program Services and Products	Total Amount Spent and Source of Funds	Cost of Service Unit*
RN or LPN visits mother and baby within 48 hours of birth	On staff currently: 2 full-time nurses and 1 part-time LPN who share visiting duties Total salary/benefits cost: $76,000 Funded by federal office of health and human services	Each nurse averages 2.8 visits per week. Total yearly visits = 437 Each visit service unit of cost = $174
Vehicle fleet	Funded by business donations	Average trip cost = $1.06
Training for nurses	3 staff receive 20 hours of training per year Total cost: $7,000 Funded by grant from St. Mary's Hospital Foundation	Training cost: $2,333 per nurse per year

County Public Health Department BabyStart Program

Program Services and Products	Total Amount Spent and Source of Funds	Cost of Service Unit
Public health nurse or RN visits mother and baby within 7 days of release from hospital	On staff currently: 9 full-time nurses Total salary/benefits cost: $270,000 Funded by county Funded by county	Nurses are expected to make 12 visits per week = 5,616 visits per year Each visit service unit of cost = $48.
Vehicle fleet	9 full-time nurses receive 20 hours of training per year	Average trip cost = $3.20
Training for the BabyStart nursing skills program	Total cost: $32,000 Funded by grant from St. Mary's Hospital Foundation	Training cost: $3,555 per nurse per year

* For both organizations, a service unit = one thirty-minute visit less than ten miles from the office.

FIGURE 5 *(continued)*

Here are questions the collaboration can ask itself about the system as it currently exists:

- The volume of visits made by the county's public health nurses helps to keep its service unit cost down. How can the collaboration partners help Clinica de la Familia—the only source of Spanish-speaking nurses—keep service unit cost down? By training public health nurses to speak Spanish? By giving some visits that would normally go to public health to Clinica de la Familia? What other ways could these agencies share tasks and costs . . . Data collection? Reporting?

- The vehicle cost for Clinica de la Familia is very low. Can businesses be persuaded to support the vehicle costs for the public health nursing program?

- The training for all the nurses probably includes common topics. Can training activities be coordinated to contain costs for all?

Each executive shares his or her three-column page with the other executives. Thus, they can compare financial information program-to-program across agencies. Who has the best value for the dollar? How do value systems or philosophies about service quality impact the unit of service cost?

Sharing this data without judging it or demanding changes (yet) is also a great way to build trust. With this data, the executives of the collaboration partners can talk oranges-to-oranges and apples-to-apples about resource use. Note that this degree of sharing does not happen often. Yet experience has shown that collaborations that bring openness to their work make deeper, more effective changes in the system, frequently finding ways to improve services. They also find it easier to put funding proposals together to make these changes possible.

A blank form, Program Financial Information, is provided in Appendix A if your collaboration decides to use this method.

Help funders understand what you need

As you learn what constitutes best practices, and as your agencies change in order to offer the best to consumers, let your funders know. Plan how your collaboration will first educate and then influence funders so they can provide the most sensible support for your work. Again, don't forget to think about the funders' self-interest. What's in this for them? And are you helping them get that?

An example of educating government funders happened in Minnesota. In an effort to integrate social services, legislators passed a law in the early 1990s that required schools, county agencies, health agencies, and human services agencies to collaborate in order to receive funding. Unwittingly, complexities in this law created trouble in local communities. People from nonprofits and other important entities, such as hospitals, ended up feeling excluded from the central decision-making table for collaborations. Local people worked hard to let their legislators hear about the conflicts that had cropped up as a result of the law. The state department responsible for carrying out the legislation lobbied also. The law was changed so that nongovernmental organizations could participate as equal partners. This promoted more effective collaborations.

This kind of give-and-take is also becoming more prevalent with foundations. More and more, private funders are inviting interactions that help them improve their funding practices for collaborations.

Begin joint budget planning as soon as possible

The third or fourth year of a collaboration (assuming the work is getting positive results) is not too early to begin joint budget meetings. Each agency involved in the collaboration will always have its own budget and its own resources. But if everybody knows what everybody else's budget plans are, this information can leverage the collaboration craftily. The following story offers a case in point:

> Bob left the collaboration partners meeting with his head down and his mouth shut. He and the four other executive directors and senior administrators had just finished their first meeting for sharing financial information. Bob wasn't embarrassed as much as he was worried. In his organization, each unit of service cost the agency $25. Two of the other organizations had a service unit cost under $17. How did they do that, he wondered, and still keep their quality up? Those agencies had great reputations for service.

> When Bob got back to his office, he had a long talk with his agency's program manager representative to the collaboration. Bob instructed her to find out how those service unit costs were kept so low. During the next twelve months, she and Bob had a series of meetings and they found four different ways to trim costs.

> Of course, on a personal level, the best part of Bob's effort was the payoff the following year. He attended the second financial meeting with proof of his new, lower service unit cost. People were impressed at how much he had accomplished. When somebody suggested they begin trying to plan budgets on the same cycle, Bob was relaxed and confident. He knew

his agency would indeed be better off in its own planning and budgeting cycle if it knew what the other agencies were doing.

His colleague, LeAndra, was less certain. "You want me to come here with my budget projections and tell you how much money I'm looking to get, where it will come from, and how I'm going to spend it? Sounds like that's great for you, but I feel like I'm giving away state secrets!"

Bob promptly replied, "No, there's very little risk for you. We can't and don't want to change how you spend your resources." (At least, not yet, he thought.) "But knowing how much lower your unit cost of service was than mine really drove me to improve the bottom line at my place. Sharing this information can really help us."

Another colleague piped up: "Besides, remember two years ago when we submitted competing grants to the Gotham Foundation and didn't even know it? We were really embarrassed when Gotham called us both in."

LeAndra paused. There could be benefits to shaping her own agency's budget in light of what other people were doing. After all, she had a new programming idea and she was looking for money to support it.

Collaboration is an opportunity to fund revisions to your agency's strategic plan and budget—an opportunity to see how your agency should change in the context of the system as a whole. And, after all, the funders of your collaborative effort expect you to integrate what you have discovered into your standing financial plan.

Funding drives programming. Funding drives product. Funding drives service. Whether you offer a museum to the public, recreation activities for kids, or new job development to a municipality, your business is based on funding. You can't change the system for the better unless you change the way it uses its resources. Take a deep breath: You may have to revise your budget in order to be the best organization you can be for your customers and for the community.

Action Step

In preparation for your next round of grantwriting, begin to develop coordinated budget-planning cycles. Have each partner bring in service unit costs for their part in the collaboration, let your funders know what you will need, and begin the hard work of planning your budgets together. If helpful, use the form Program Financial Information in Appendix A. Collaborations involved in large efforts to solve complex issues should also see the section Use a community-driven process to distribute funds, pages 100–102. Nimble collaborations recognize the need to shift traditional funding patterns in ways that improve the system. Being nimble doesn't mean just being quick. Such funding fixes take years . . . and nimble collaborations have the resilience to stay the course for the good of their communities.

Create a Nimble Governance System

A *governance system* is the set of policies, procedures, systems, and cultural norms that define the work processes among partners. It's the way you and your partners guide, direct, and make decisions. Governance will emerge naturally; there is no such thing as a group without governance. But the wise collaboration shapes its governance deliberately. Many collaborations already use an organizational chart to illustrate their governance system. These charts tend to look similar to Figures 3 and 4, which describe democratic and diffuse decision-making styles (pages 59 and 60). However, these charts do not fully describe the governance system.

A *governance agreement* more completely documents the governance system. It acts as a contract (sometimes legal, sometimes less formal) and answers questions that will come up as you and your partners collaborate. It can quiet anxiety about how decisions will be made and who will be responsible for what actions. Governance agreements often state the mission and vision of the collaboration, and then describe details about desired results, decision-making processes, finances, insurance and liability assignments, data privacy, and so on.

Ten years ago no precedents for creating such agreements existed. Today the question is, "Which precedent will work best for us and our partners?" Get sample legal agreements from your county attorney's office, or seek out agreements from similar collaborations in your state. Another option is to use the forms Write a Memo of Agreement for Your Collaboration and Draft a Formal Governance Agreement in Appendix A as a template for your collaboration's agreement.

There is one key to keeping your collaboration legal *and* nimble: *Create only the documents you need.* Only you and your partners know what legal concerns you must deal with as a collaboration. Reaching agreement on issues like insurance, liability exposure, data privacy, and regulations for an integrated fund resides in each state's laws. Contact your county attorney or the legal staff at your state departments for sample agreements. Keep the documentation as simple as possible.

Remember that not every collaboration needs a legal agreement. Unless required by law or by common sense, don't waste time writing agreements, bylaws, or complicated contracts. Many collaborations get sidetracked and postpone the real work

i

Unless required by law or by common sense, don't waste time writing agreements, bylaws, or complicated contracts . . . . If the partners in the collaboration just keep talking about what they will do, they'll never have to get down and do it.

because they're wordsmithing "bylaws." If the partners in the collaboration just keep talking about what they will do, they'll never have to get down and do it.

You can use three steps to document your governance system: write, revise, and renew. These steps will take you from a relatively simple memo of agreement to a more complete and formal governance agreement.

Step 1: Write

Most collaborations write an initial "memo of agreement" early on in their partnership. The process of drafting and approving such a memo builds buy-in and support from individual agencies and establishes a firm foundation that can sustain a collaborative effort over time.

Unless a specific contract is required by law, the simpler your first agreement, the better. Many collaborations never write a more formal document. They simply revise the memos year after year, clarifying their agreement and getting more sophisticated letters signed by each partner organization.

The form Write a Memo of Agreement for Your Collaboration in Appendix A shows a memo from one partner, the Community Garden, to other partners in the Playspace Collaboration. If your collaboration has not already done so, collect this kind of memo from each partner organization, and then assemble the copies. Share this collection of memos with all the other partners so that each agency can see what the other agencies have written.

An important part of this process is to ask each agency to create its own version of the agreement. Don't create a template for board chairs to sign. Instead, list the elements the memo might contain, and encourage the board to discuss these items and write its own memo. Elements most often found in a memo of agreement include

- A list of the partners that your leadership or board believes is participating in the effort
- A description of the vision and mission that drives the collaboration
- A description of the outcomes or results that the collaboration wants to achieve, and your board's commitment to getting those results
- A statement of your organization's self-interest and, if possible, a statement of resources that your organization is prepared to dedicate to the effort

Discussing this list ensures that the top leaders of the partner organizations fully understand what the collaboration is about. It also ensures that they have started to wrestle with the notion that they may be asked to change their organizations in some way.

Established collaborations no doubt already have some form of governance agreement. Such collaborations can skip this step and move to Step 2, which involves assembling and organizing other documents that the collaboration has produced.

Step 2: Revise

The next step in developing a nimble governance agreement is to collect and review the documents the collaboration has been creating. These documents define what the collaboration is all about: memos of agreement, vision statement, lists of desired results, and so forth. In this step, the collaboration inventories its best work in order to develop a sense of "self." A governance agreement based on these documents helps cement into place what is best about the way partners work together—a key element of sustainability. These documents

- Solidify agreements about the results the collaboration wants—and sustain the partners' energy for achieving those results

- Build trust and strengthen relationships between organizations

- Ensure that the collaboration is operating on the ten principles of resilience

Listed below are common documents that collaborations create and confirm with each partner as the collaboration develops. The documents are listed in the order that they are usually developed, but don't worry if your collaboration doesn't follow this progression. With each type of document, a list of examples is provided, as well as a list of the questions the documents answer for the collaboration. Remember, these written pages substaniate your results, relationships, and resilience.

Statements of results

Examples: vision statement, mission statement, memos that agree to outcomes and evaluation criteria, initial work plan, memos from agencies accepting their responsibilities in the work plan.

Questions answered: What promise are partners making to consumers, constituents, and staff? What is the vision and mission of the collaboration? How does the mission of individual organizations play into this partnership? What specific outcomes are we working on? How will we evaluate the outcomes? What tasks will we do, and who will perform them? Who is accountable for what? How do we change activities that aren't working for us? Should we hire a coordinator? When will we renew the work plan? How will we know when we've successfully changed the system—and that we can dismantle the collaboration?

Role descriptions

Examples: memos that describe the responsibilities of each organization in the collaboration, job descriptions for individuals who attend collaboration meetings, a job description for the coordinator, if there is one.

Questions answered: Why are these agencies at the table? What do they want from this (self-interest)? What can they contribute? Does each agree to consider changing itself for the betterment of the whole system? Does the agency representative have the power to make decisions for his or her agency? Does the agency representative agree to champion our work back at his or her office? How do we get tasks done? Who is responsible for what portion of our work together? Who has power? How do we attain power equity between "little" organizations and "big" organizations? Which organization leads, and when does it lead? What is the role of the coordinator?

Policies for decision making

Examples: memos that describe the responsibilities of each organization in the collaboration, decision-making trees, conflict-management protocols, a schedule for eliminating the coordinator's job description, if the collaboration has decided to do without a coordinator.

Questions answered: Do we all need to make all decisions together? What can we delegate? How do we know the best decision has been made? What if it turns out to be a bad decision? How do we resolve conflict? What is our coordinator's role in making decisions? How long will we need a coordinator?

Legal documents

Examples: contracts, application forms, insurance forms, liability assignments and/or risk assessments, data-privacy protocols, supervision standards for the coordinator, if there is one.

Questions answered: How formal do our written agreements need to be? How do we handle liability issues? Data privacy? Are there legal mandates to consider as we work? How will the coordinator be evaluated?

Financial agreements

Examples: fiscal policies, joint budgets.

Questions answered: What should our fiscal agent be doing? Who can spend money? Should we be looking for new resources or redistributing the resources at hand? How do we apply for grants?

Changes to the system

Examples: lists of "lessons learned," revisions to standard operating procedures and job descriptions, revised memos of agreement, work plans for the second and following years of the collaboration, the budgets from each organization in the collaboration.

Questions answered: How can individual agencies change the way they work in order to improve the collaboration? How can the organizations absorb the coordinator's functions? How can we apply the lessons learned so far from this collaboration? How can we modify the collaboration structure, fiscal agreements, and task accountability based on the results of our evaluation? How will each agency absorb the costs of changing the way business is done? How can we embed the collaboration's vision into the vision of individual agencies? Should we select a "champion" to keep the vision of this collaboration alive?

Celebrations

Examples: thank-you letters, lists of changes that organizations have made, histories of the collaboration, public relations plans, marketing plans.

Questions answered: How can we highlight our successes? How can we thank our partner organizations and clients?

Step 3: Renew

In Step 3, you write a formal governance agreement. The agreement itself should be built from the documents you've assembled. It should be general enough to allow for flexibility, but it should make the vision, desired results, evaluation measurements, and other aspects of the collaboration's "culture" clear, so that partners can come and go nimbly while the work of the collaboration remains constant.

Once this document has been created, the collaboration should review and amend it annually or biannually.

The form Draft a Formal Governance Agreement in Appendix A shows a simple example. Your collaboration may be required to have a formal governance agreement in place by the laws that mandated your collaboration. Or, you and your partners may want a formal interagency agreement in order to make funding easier, cement your relationships, and sustain your collaborative effort over time. Interagency governance agreements vary widely from state to state. The information provided here is intended to help you think about the governance agreement you need, but it is not complete. Check with your state's attorney general or your collaboration's funder for specific information.

Action Step

Create (or revise) a governance agreement and put it in writing.

Avoid nonprofit status for your collaboration

Some people believe a collaboration should become a nonprofit organization (a 501(c)(3) organization) in order to accept grants. In most cases, nimble collaborations do not seek nonprofit status. Such status is unnecessary when one of the partners agrees to be fiscal agent and accept grants. Nonprofit status is also risky: It is an invitation to shape a new bureaucracy and thus violate a key principle of resilience.

A collaboration that seeks nonprofit status opens the door to some common problems:

Sharp reduction of funds spent on clients. An organization costs money to run, and that money comes out of the grants you write. As much as 30 percent of grant money can be siphoned off to pay for 501(c)(3) auditors, office expenses, stationery, and related expenses. The point of collaboration is to establish permanent relationships, not permanent offices.

Wider distances in relationships. When collaborations incorporate as nonprofits, partners play the role of "board member" of the 501(c)(3), not the role of partner or peer. Many people naturally assume that the executive director or staff of the 501(c)(3) will do all the work. The fabric of partner-to-partner interaction frays.

New player syndrome. The collaboration coordinator becomes the new executive director of the 501(c)(3). The coordinator's initiative and hard work grow an expanded agency. Soon, the collaboration "nonprofit agency" has its hand in all sorts of work and all sorts of pots. The new agency can even be perceived as a competitor to existing agencies, causing great conflict.

A new nonprofit organization can become another expensive roadblock to systems innovation and a barrier to nimble responses in changing circumstances. Avoid becoming a nonprofit, 501(c)(3) if you possibly can.

Chapter Summary

Every collaboration faces the challenges of sustaining its work over time so it can achieve the results it wants. The nimble collaboration relies on the tactics in this chapter: The collaboration actively employs the ten principles of resilience, and it builds decision-making and governance structures to support those principles. Nimble collaborations share pertinent financial information as early as trust allows, and begin to plan future budgets to allow for the changes each partner agency must make. Finally, the nimble collaboration documents its structure and obtains signed memos of agreement or other governance documentation from each partner.

Part I of this book has investigated how the strategies of results, relationships, and resiliency can make collaborations deft, flexible, sustainable, and responsive—in a word, nimble. In Part II we'll see how these strategies play out in real-life collaborations facing real-life work. Chapters Four and Five describe two typical collaborations, service integration collaborations and complex problem-solving collaborations, with attention to how these collaborations can be nimble.

This chart summarizes the actions suggested in Chapters One–Three of this book. To be deft and innovative, the nimble collaboration takes actions focused on results, rela-

Results

- *Determine premise of the work*

  At the next meeting of collaborative partners, decide which premise best describes your current activities: coordination, cooperation, or collaboration.

- *Determine the promise of the work*

  Decide what results you are promising to whom, and write them down.

- *Describe mission and vision*

  Plan time to revisit the collaboration mission statement and vision statement whenever new partners are added or when an evaluation cycle is completed.

- *Define outcomes*

  Write outcome statements that will bring you close to your mission and vision. Use these statements actively during your meetings and for making decisions.

Relationships

- *Build trust*

  Put an open discussion of self-interests on the agenda for an upcoming collaboration meeting. In six months, put it on the agenda again and see if self-interests are clearer or, perhaps, have changed.

- *Analyze membership*

  Discuss the current representation in your collaboration. Is every group that is part of the system—the solution or the problem—represented in some form?

- *Map membership*

  Create a membership ring for your collaboration that involves the right organizations at the right time in the right activities.

- *Assign roles to members*

  State clearly the role that each partner plays, allowing the flexibility to change roles as needed. Layer meetings to help people with similar roles work together.

Resilience

- *Advance sustainability*

  Ask senior managers and boards of partner agencies to discuss the implications of the ten principles of resilience for the collaborative effort, and for their individual organizations.

- *Diffuse decision making*

  Put your protocol for making decisions in writing and ask core members to sign off on it. Whenever a task is assigned, be sure it includes a list of the results desired from any decision, and assign level 1, level 2, or level 3 to that decision.

Nimble Collaboration

tionships, and resilience. The action steps listed are not a step-by-step prescription for nimbleness, but rather a compendium of ways to meet challenges and to be successful.

• *Evaluate*
Put a half-day retreat on the calendar for all the partners in the collaboration to celebrate any positive evaluation of outcomes or to evaluate the collaboration process itself.

• *Deal with pilot projects*
Actively review the reason you are setting up any "pilot projects." Why are they needed? When will the project cease being a pilot and be implemented across the board?

• *Change the system*
Consider which best practices are ready to be incorporated as standard operating procedures (SOPs) within each partner agency. Set a deadline for meeting to share these changes in SOPs among members of the collaboration.

• *Reduce need for coordinator*
Look hard at the work your collaboration coordinator is doing. Should the partners themselves do any of that work? What will the collaboration do when there are no funds for the coordinator's position?

• *Discuss progress at home office*
Add a standing item to your collaboration meeting agendas: Find out how members are championing the work of the collaboration within their organizations.

• *Promote customer involvement*
Find effective ways to involve end users. Do not ask customers and consumers to sit through meetings that do not interest them.

• *Promote funder involvement*
Find effective ways to involve funders. Keep funders apprised of the collaboration's progress, and consider whether they should be involved in a more active way.

• *Streamline communications*
Design a communications system that's sensitive to agency placement in the membership ring. Communicate only what is essential to each role.

• *Gain financial support*
Begin to coordinate the budget-planning cycles for partner organizations.

• *Create or confirm a governance agreement*
Create (or revise) your governance agreement and put it in writing.

PART II

Applying Nimble Strategies to Real-Life Collaborations

There are many different types of collaborations. Two of the most common are those created to integrate services and those created to address a broad, complex problem or challenge, such as widespread violence, increasing urban green space, or economic revitalization.

The former of these two collaborations (*service integration*) may stand alone. However, it is sometimes a single strategy among many strategies used in the latter (*complex issue resolution*). For example, a metropolitan region that is working to reduce violence might include as one of its strategies the integration of intake procedures at domestic abuse shelters. In fact, such a collaboration may have a number of service integration strategies going on, as well as many other strategies.

Because service integration can be a step in resolving a complex issue, it is covered first, in Chapter Four. Complex issue resolution is dealt with in Chapter Five. Throughout, you will see how the strategies for becoming nimble apply to these typical collaborations.

Chapter Four

Collaborate to Integrate Services

Collaboration offers a method for moving organizations out of isolated positions where they serve customers but remain ignorant of their counterparts in the community. Efforts to integrate services are occurring in social services, arts, health care, economic development, housing, and education, to name a few. This chapter explores important ways to get results, promote positive relationships, and build resiliency into your efforts to integrate services. As noted in the introduction to Part II, service integration may stand alone or be part of a larger effort to address a complex issue—the topic of Chapter Five. Be sure to review Chapter Five for best practices in addressing complex issues; here we will pay special attention to the techniques collaborations can use to keep service integration going.

Service integration is an umbrella phrase that includes efforts sometimes termed *wrap-around service delivery, unified case management,* and *service reinvention.* The basic philosophy driving these changes is to deal with all aspects of a service consumer's situation rather than deal with problems in a piecemeal fashion. Other motivations for service integration include the wise use of resources, the desire to empower the client, continual improvement of practices, and the need to use outcome-based evaluations that measure real results for consumers. For example:

> A development of new homes in a midwestern community is committed to helping low-income people buy homes of their own. This particular development—a campus of 115 town homes, a recreation center, and a regional library with a satellite office of county social services—is owned and operated by the federal office of Housing and Urban Development. During the last few years, service providers on this campus have worked hard to provide a vast array of services to town home residents in an easily accessible, seamless style. Today, families that move into a town home fill out a single information packet. That information is shared (through Internet and computer technology) with county assistance

offices, public health nurses, and the local schools, if the family has school-aged children. A resident can get food stamps, help with heating bills, placement into the library's English class, employment referrals, and an appointment with the local clinic to get immunizations for kids in school. All these services are available without filling out new intake forms once the first packet is complete. Residents may request an advocate who helps them navigate the web of services and opportunities on campus and in the general community.

From clients' viewpoints, service integration means several things:

- They don't have to go from building to building and person to person to try to garner the health and social supports, education, or recreation services they need.

- There are multiple channels for securing products and services.

- Information is collected and provided in a consistent format and available through a host of providers. Computer technology is used to keep client information in a single account that runs across agencies.

- Clients can act in a self-sufficient manner and be more responsible for the social supports they use.

Service integration requires a nimble collaboration for a number of reasons, and two are especially important.

First, the final authority to run public systems resides with public officials, and the authority to run private systems resides with private authorities. Public health departments, school districts, protection services for children, and human services are all agencies whose authority is vested in elected officials. In contrast, the source of authority for a nongovernmental organization is its board of directors. To integrate services across sectors, these directors must lead in tandem with elected officials in public systems. Collaborations can support this process and help all leaders manage resources appropriately. By paying attention to the strategies for being nimble, collaborations involved in service integration can keep the work moving and avoid getting lost among all the bureaucratic systems in which they operate.

Second, the expertise for creating an integrated system is widely dispersed. This means all the players in the system must share information and insights. System users, professional providers, constituents, stakeholders—all these people need a collection point for dialogue, a place to plot and rearrange the individual parts of the system. A service integration collaboration provides such a collection point.[15]

---

[15] Gary Cox, "Model Agreement for Children's Collaboratives in Minnesota" (St. Paul, MN: Minnesota Department of Human Services, Jan. 1998).

Integrating services for families—some emerging models

The desire for a coordinated access system for all families reaches across organizations and geography. Below is a brief synopsis of a few possible models that partnerships and collaborations are implementing across the United States.[16]

211. This is a national abbreviated phone number that gives constituents free access to human services and health information. The United Way of Metropolitan Atlanta first created and implemented the use of this number. Like 911, 211 is an easy-to-recognize phone number that helps link families to the information and services they need. At this time, the number is under discussion or being implemented in many states.

Central Administration Community Information Program. The Community Information Program (CIP) is a program of the Peninsula Library System, a consortium of public and community college libraries in San Mateo County, California. With a computerized human services database, CIP provides information on more than 7,500 private nonprofit agencies, government programs, and community organizations. CIP also helps human services professionals locate and manage resource information and find networking meetings and training opportunities.

Kiosks. In Delaware, a computer kiosk system provides consumers with information on available services, such as job search office locations and phone numbers. Individuals touch the display panel to find information about their particular area of interest which they are then able to print out. Information is available in both English and Spanish.

SMART Cards. SMART Cards are currently being used by a variety of social services agencies in California. These cards store personal information or data on a small card. This information can then be accessed, downloaded, and updated by multiple organizations. Some information on the cards can be restricted to maintain confidentiality.

One Ease E-Link. One Ease E-Link (OEL) is currently being implemented in New Jersey. The New Jersey Department of Health and Senior Services, the Department of Human Services, and the Department of Labor jointly sponsor this program. (However, each organization is responsible for the management of its network.) This program offers new ways of finding out about client eligibility for social services and identifying appropriate providers—all via computer networks. OEL also offers a forum for individuals to ask questions and obtain information on important issues. Basically, this program is creating an online business environment for social services agencies.

Online Automated Service Integration System (OASIS). OASIS is a referral system used by social work professionals. It ensures that clients who come to Delaware Health and Social Services are served in an efficient and effective manner. This software also helps ensure that clients are referred to the correct service, regardless of their first contact point. In addition, the program tracks clients who are being served by multiple divisions.

---

[16] Compiled by Jessica Parker-Carlson et al., *Points of Access Research Report* (Anoka, MN: Anoka County Children and Family Council, 2001), 13.

Know When You're Really Working on Service Integration

Many collaborations call themselves *service integration collaborations*, but the words have become jargon and their definitions have become muddied. Let's be sure of our terms.

A collaboration is aimed at service integration if the partners are engaged in two or more of these activities:

- It focuses on clients who are engaged in two or more agencies at a time—for instance, teens who are working with a school social worker and who are under case management by a parole officer.
- It seeks to improve the service system it is in (kids, arts, health care, employment) by reducing duplication of services, programs, or planning activities.
- It seeks to improve the service system it is in by sorting out fragmented services and filling in gaps in services and programs.
- It wants to access resources wisely, including working with funders more closely and seeking out underused resources in the community.
- It aspires to unified case management, wrap-around services, seamless service, or any of the current best practices in which organizations plan and deliver services together.
- It includes agencies and organizations that the partners have not worked with previously.

In contrast, a collaboration is *not* seeking service integration collaboration if it does any of the following:

- It is working on a limited task that does not include addressing system issues.
- Most partners show up at a collaboration meeting because somebody else got some grant money, or it looks like somebody's going to get some kind of funding.
- The law mandates that the agencies be part of a collaboration, but the agencies do not complete the internal work necessary to be effective partners.
- Mandated collaboration or not, the agencies at the table privately assure themselves that they aren't going to do anything differently.
- The agencies view the collaborative effort as a "special project" to run alongside their normal operations for as long as the grant money lasts.

Recognize Three Points of Service Integration

Collaborations can work to integrate services in many different ways. The three most common efforts expand collaboration at one of these three different intersections between service and consumer:

Service integration at the point of service access. This is often called "no wrong door" or "streamlined access," making it easy for people to find the service they want. Most often this service integration work focuses on marketing, information, and referral mechanisms.

Service integration at the point of intake and assessment. Many organizations use the same intake form, subcontract assessment services through the same vendor, or use some other device so that families most likely to need more than one service do not have to go through separate intake processes with each provider.

Collaboration mystery revealed

Service integration isn't a project you undertake; it's a commitment you make.

Service integration at the point of service delivery. Wrap-around service or unified case management eliminates duplication of service during the time the consumer is engaged. There are usually protocols in place to describe when a consumer has completed the work.

It's important to distinguish these three points of integration because some are easier to establish than others, and all three require different skills from collaborating organizations.

The key question to ask is, "What service integration effort makes the most sense for our constituents and our community organizations?" Following are some answers, including "dos and don'ts" relevant to each point of integration.

Integration at the point of service access

The first of the three intersections between service and consumer is the point where consumers access service. This is the easiest place for all service providers in the community to work together. Everyone benefits. Often the results include improved service directories or improved protocols for referring clients from agency to agency. Such results are illustrated in the following example:

> In 2000, a large suburban county in the Midwest researched its provider community. The research was conducted by the county's Children and Family Council, whose mission is to "nurture collaborative efforts by building bridges and networks between people and agencies that share a

vision of a healthier community for children and families." The collaborative was the obvious body for exploring how community residents find and access family support services.

Prior to the research, any discussions regarding the current system of access relied on personal experience and anecdotal evidence. In its research, the council described the current access system from the service providers' point of view. Researchers surveyed or talked to hundreds of staff members from school districts, county human services, public health, nonprofit organizations, community action programs, and other organizations.

The research showed that according to the service providers, county residents received information about the services they needed from referral sources. Whether from a family friend, a school social worker, or a printed brochure, consumers went to at least two sources for help. In other words, most often people knocked on the wrong door the first time and then were sent to the right agency. The research also showed that referrals were followed up on only about 10 percent of the time. In other words, providers did not know if families were eventually connected to the help they needed or if the families just gave up.

This county has received funding from a foundation and is undergoing a vigorous redesign of its information and referral systems with plenty of input from consumers.[17]

The county in this example is not unique. Most consumers across the nation have little understanding of the service community, and neither do the ministers, teachers, family members, and other people they turn to for help. If your collaboration is working on integrating service at this intersection, consider the following dos and don'ts of service integration.

Do work with an established collaboration whose mission is streamlining service for citizens

Service integration collaborations will pay off faster if they start from the foundation of an existing group. Such a group already has the stated agenda of modifying existing services, so members are more likely to examine recommendations for systems change.

Do build information technology quickly

With appropriate computers and information systems, you can create service directories that are easy to use and easy to keep current. These information systems can be modified gradually to make and follow up on specific referrals, or to do other tasks related to service integration. Many small nongovernmental organizations are important members of the service community, but they don't have the resources to buy

---

[17] Information adapted from Parker-Carlson et al., *Points of Access Research Report.*

and upgrade hardware and software. Use your collaboration to make these resources available to them.

Recently, the Oregon Department of Human Services conducted an assessment of service integration needs. The department found that the most often requested tools and systems supported information sharing and common case planning between partners, including technology systems for

- Sharing common demographic data
- Seeing what other agencies or partners a client is involved with
- Supporting common case planning[18]

Don't work on common marketing strategies first

Most of the work at this intersection should focus on polishing up and enhancing referral systems, not marketing. Many organizations are already trying to keep up with their existing caseload, and marketing can only increase the backlog. The idea here is not to overlook people who need help, but to be ready to serve them seamlessly and effectively. Referral systems that work should be in place before enhancing marketing materials. Then organizations will be ready to serve more people more efficiently, and marketing can be appropriate.

Don't forget the human element

Referral networks are built on a person-to-person basis. A staff person's tenure and personal connections can be the most important element in good referral processes. Does every organization in your collaboration use similar referral protocols? Does every worker in every school district, government agency, and nonprofit office have

A true fable . . . Marketing mishap makes many mad

A midwestern collaboration was so proud of itself. It finally found the resources it needed to publish all of its marketing materials, such as brochures and flyers and web sites, in Spanish as well as English. The collaborating agencies knew there was a large seasonal influx of Spanish-speaking migrant workers as well as an established Hispanic community in the area's biggest town, so they thought bilingual marketing materials were important.

Soon after the bilingual publication of an important report, agency phones began ringing. "Hola, hola" the caller would say—and stunned agency operators realized there were no interpreters or Spanish-speaking staff in the office. The collaboration had built a market it could not serve.

---

[18] Terry Guza et al., *OIS Service Integration Needs Assessment Project, Final Report* (Portland, OR: Oregon Department of Human Services, May 2001).

access to an up-to-date resource directory? Do collaboration partners have the capacity to follow up on every referral they make? These human elements must be in place in order for service integration to work at the intersection of consumer and access point.

Integration at the point of intake and assessment

The second intersection between service and consumer is the point where consumers undergo intake and assessment. Many collaborations set up a subgroup for integrated intake and assessment, since the services are required for a limited number of families in any community. Referral systems can help anyone—for example, healthy families looking for recreation or individuals looking for occupational training. But integrated intake and assessment services focus on people or families involved with more than one agency. This fact often requires a subgroup of a collaboration to build systems that respond to challenges. Here are a few suggestions for "nimble-izing" collaborations that are integrating intake and assessment.

Do start with a limited number of families or challenges

You can experience collaboration success at the outset by doing integrated intake and assessment for a limited number of clients. Possible examples include children in out-of-home placement because the mother is unemployed and chemically dependent, or teenagers on parole who need help to stay in school. This will not be a pilot project, because you will be changing the system in all the ways explained in this book. You are simply working on a smaller pool of potential system barriers and learning how to be nimble. After a year or two of limited work, begin expanding joint intake and assessment to other consumers.

Do deal directly with confidentiality issues

Client confidentiality is one of the key perceived barriers to integrating intake and assessment systems. According to the Oregon Department of Human Services, views on confidentiality fall into two camps: (1) those who believe confidentiality is essential because it protects the client from potential exploitation through misuse of personal information, and (2) those who believe that most client information (with the exception of some treatment and diagnosis specifics) can be shared in the client's best interests. The department, in examining the issue further, found that "where a common release form . . . was in place, with the partners listed on the form . . . clients seldom refused to sign the form. Generally clients wanted to get all of the possible assistance to resolve their problem and understood, in fact welcomed, the partners working together."[19]

Reassure all partners in the collaboration that legal barriers to such integration can be overcome and should be actively explored. The problem can be resolved as the collaboration clarifies its values and carefully documents its decisions and procedures.

---

[19] Guza et al., *OIS Service Integration Needs Assessment Project.*

Don't be fooled by a one-stop shop approach

Placing all the family support organizations in your community in a single building makes it easy for consumers to receive integrated assessment. But the downsides of building a central location are considerable. Tension can arise among the collaborative partners—those that office together, and those that don't. Clients face the stigma of going to the "bad-family" building. And the amount of effort it takes to move agencies into a single campus is exhausting. Also, the smallest agencies find that keeping their own stand-alone site and operating an office at a shared location is prohibitively expensive. Staff at the shared location may develop "tunnel vision" and forget the resources offered by other members of the collaboration who don't have an office at the shared site. Similarly, one-stop shops may overlook other allied agencies that are important to the community, like the library, the YMCA, or service clubs, which all will continue to have stand-alone sites.

Of course, one-stop shops can be effective, nimble collaborations. But it's important to remember that one-stop shops may be successfully implemented using cooperative and coordinated strategies instead of more complicated collaborative strategies. (See pages 15-19 for a discussion of the cooperate-coordinate-collaborate continuum.) Collaborations that create virtual one-stop shops can be an innovative alternative. Your collaboration can use information technology to create common databases, client screening and assessment tools, and tracking systems. Change the expectations for caseworkers, giving them the resources they need to meet often with caseworkers from other agencies. Set hours for caseworkers when families are available. Send caseworkers to meet with clients in libraries, schools, and businesses. The money you save in planning and creating a one-stop shop can be poured into the technology that works for integrating assessment.

> **Collaboration mystery revealed**
>
> The point of collaboration is to establish permanent relationships, not permanent offices.

The exception to this "don't" is for collaborations in large urban areas. Here, the service system is so complex that most collaborations rarely include all the players. There have been successful attempts to create neighborhood-based service centers or welcome centers in cities such as St. Paul, Minnesota. A lot of what families need is available at these centers, and a strong referral network connects them to other support services.

Integration at the point of service delivery

The third intersection between service and consumer is at the moment of actual service delivery. Integrated service delivery may involve unified case management for one person or for every member of the family. Many members of the collaboration may want to be involved, and the family itself may take an active role in service planning. For example:

> Bob and Betty had been divorced about four years. Bob tried to send regular child support to Betty and the kids, but frequent layoffs and other job problems interfered. Betty had become increasingly depressed over the last few months and seldom left the house anymore. When the kids started acting out in school, the social worker from the unified case management team visited Betty at home. After the whole family attended a couple of assessment sessions, it was time to get Bob to job training, Betty to a counselor, and the kids to after-school recreation activities. Betty's mom offered to help by providing daycare for the kids two Saturdays a month.

To integrate services at the point of service delivery, learn about best practices for unified case management and train individual workers in team processes. Reengineer standard operating procedures to work toward integrated service delivery. Following are tips for integrating service delivery.

Do focus on results, relationships, and resiliency

All of the principles and techniques for building nimble collaborations work in service integration collaborations. Use this book and all the other resources available to you to work nimbly toward individual agency renewal and systems change.

Do involve the state department leaders

The often-invisible-800-pound gorillas in this work are the state and federal departments that provide the big intervention services: the departments of social services, employment, education, housing, economic development, and public health, for instance. A service integration collaboration must incorporate these partners effectively. Work out an action plan that helps them represent their services powerfully and positively. Will the collaboration be applying for rules waivers? Many states are trying to pilot service integration in selective ways. Is there funding and support for the local effort?

Do structure the unified case management teams for accountability and flexibility

In a nimble collaboration focused on unified case management, the most appropriate model for decision making can be diagrammed as a target. This target resembles the model used in Chapter Two to describe memberships of the collaboration. Do you see the theme? The clients and the key results the collaboration seeks sit in the center of the diagram. The farther an agency is from the center, the farther it is from accountability for those results. Refer to the details in Figure 6: Target Structure for Service Integration Collaborations, on the following page, to see how this works.

Figure 6: Target Structure for Service Integration Collaborations

The eighth principle of resilience demands that collaborations push decision making down as close to the consumer as possible. (See page 57.) In the center of this figure—the bull's-eye—are clients. Staff involved in unified case management realize they are creating the best possible action or treatment plan for the *client*, not for a particular agency. Everyone acknowledges that clients hold the most power and accountability for getting the results they want. This model for service integration endorses a powerful, client-centered approach to case management.

The first ring beyond the bull's-eye—where direct service staff reside—reflects the decision-making power of those staff. This is central to the notion of nimbleness: Those people or agencies most accountable for obtaining results for the clients or consumers get the most decision-making power. These staff members help the client create a useful action or treatment plan that taps all of the resources in the system. Direct service staff often best understand how the system works and can most easily identify the barriers to good interagency client service and how to overcome them. Clients and staff find ways to integrate funding and save money by reducing duplication. Wise collaborations give the unified teams budgets to work from so that they can even make decisions about how much to spend on which clients.

Occasionally the direct service workers will bump up against a decision they are not sure they can or should make, so they ask their program managers to get involved—the second ring beyond the bull's-eye. Nimble collaborations ask people at the same level of power across organizations to work together, so the direct service staff meet with one another (and the client) and the program managers they report to also meet together as a group. Program managers get involved in one of two ways: when individual direct service staff go to their managers for a decision, or when program managers from the partner agencies work together in a team approach. Program managers from different agencies can meet as a team to resolve the issues that frontline staff cannot. Budget dilemmas often get resolved here. Program managers are also responsible for tracking client outcomes and publishing the results of the innovations the collaboration is making.

About 80 percent of the decision making is handled at the first and second rings. Once in a while, these groups will uncover a policy change that needs to come from people higher up in their organizations. This is the third ring out. Senior administrators may be involved in some decisions, depending on the size of the agency and the level of decision-making power each agency gives its administrators. Agency boards are called on when an organization policy prohibits effective interagency work. Board members may also be asked to use their political influence to promote the collaboration or to intervene during a difficult conflict. Elected officials and board members are expected to modify funding plans and influence funding streams to support new ways of doing business.

Integrated or unified case management is the heart and soul of a collaboration attempting to deeply change the system of service delivery. When such a collaboration structures teams successfully, the people involved in the system get the information they need when they need it. As an example, consider the following case study, which shows how a client-centered structure was able to successfully serve a teen who needed help finishing school and staying sober. While reading this case study, look for ways in which the partners used the strategies of results, relationships, and resilience in order to respond nimbly to emerging situations.

Case study: Teen moves from addiction treatment to school

Dan (from corrections), Beth (from social services), and Ly (from school district support services) form a unified case management team for kids being mainstreamed back into school after alcohol or drug treatment. The nearby Big Woods Teen Treatment Center handles 80 percent of the teens from the three local high schools who have been committed for treatment. Dan, Beth, and Ly meet with the teen and her parents to devise plans for ensuring the child's successful transition back to high school and subsequent follow-up care.

One day the trio took on a new client, Alice, who had responded very well to addiction treatment. They thought they would be handling Alice's case in the standard way. As soon as the meeting started, Alice spoke up. "Let me tell you what I liked best about the treatment center."

Dan interrupted, taking charge of the conversation. "We're not looking back at treatment, Alice. We're looking forward to your return to high school."

Ly looked down at his papers, hiding his disagreement with this heavy-handed approach to Alice. Dan continued to dominate the meeting, and Alice left the meeting with a traditional aftercare plan.

Later, Ly complained to Jackson, his supervisor and the vice-superintendent for support services for the district, that Dan was an "old-fashioned" caseworker who didn't really help the team be creative. Ly told Jackson of opportunities in recent cases where something new and innovative could happen for the family, but Dan quashed it.

Jackson was earnest. "These are joint case management sessions, Ly, not Dan's case management session. You must speak up. If you're afraid of embarrassing Dan, then call a break and speak to him privately. Do you know if Beth feels the same way?" The coaching session went on, and Ly promised himself to try something different.

Dan, Beth, and Ly were disappointed when Alice was referred back to the team by the school principal. Her teachers were reporting that she was alternately withdrawn or surly, and they worried that her moods forecast relapse. This time Beth started the discussion. "What's wrong, Alice? Why are your teachers telling us you're moody?"

> **Comment**
> Successful unified case management and service integration relies heavily on the relationship strategies that enable people to manage conflict. Look at the fifth principle of resilience on page 56: Conflict is expected and managed effectively. Nimble collaborations realize that they can't expect staff like Ly, Dan, and Beth to manage conflict if they don't model these skills in their partnership meetings. Spend collaboration resources on training to build skills in conducting difficult discussions.

Dan moved into the conversation. "You know relapse means going back to court, don't you, Alice?"

Beth turned to Dan calmly and asked him to let Alice speak. At first Alice wasn't very articulate; it took a while before the problem became clear. During treatment she had been rewarded for good effort with piano lessons and access to the piano for practice. She was enamored, and worked hard with a keen eye to more and more private time at the keyboard. She missed her music, her music teacher, and the outlet it seemed to provide. "I tried to tell you when we met before how important my music is to me.

Can't you get me lessons? There's an old piano in the school auditorium, but Mrs. Crenshaw said I can't use it." It didn't take long for everyone to agree that Alice's piano lessons were important for keeping her on track.

Dan and Beth turned immediately to Ly, expecting him to arrange for these lessons through the schools. Ly knew that the school's music curriculum had been whittled down during the last ten years until very little was left—mostly a teacher who coached the band. "I can talk to Mrs. Crenshaw and arrange for you to spend practice time at the piano in the auditorium," he said ruefully, "but the school has no resources for piano lessons." Ly wanted social services to pay for the lessons and began asking Beth about how they could arrange it.

"Those kinds of discretionary funds are more easily available in corrections," Beth rejoined.

Everyone looked at Dan, who was chagrined. He did not speak, but he knew his boss would laugh him out of the office. They weren't there to create another Britney Spears. They were there to keep the kid from relapse, but everybody seemed to have forgotten.

Comment

In this case, it is clear that Ly, Beth, and Dan need to push the decision out one level. The target structure (shown in Figure 6, page 91) can help frontline direct service providers in such situations. It identifies who's meeting in what team configurations to resolve issues that direct service staff cannot resolve in their unified case management meetings. Make sure your work specifies who makes what decisions and how everyone communicates. Is an e-mail OK? Whom do you send it to? These kinds of details (tied to the strategies of relationships and resilience, and embedded in the governance agreement) provide a firm foundation for a flexible response to current conditions.

It was Alice's mom who spoke next. "When we started, you told me that if the three of you couldn't solve a problem, you could call on your supervisors. Can one of them help us get piano lessons for Alice?"

Beth opened her laptop and sent a quick note from the unified case management team to Leah, the contact for the program managers team—the team of managers to whom Beth, Dan, and Ly reported. Beth's note asked that the program managers resolve this problem in their next meeting. The rest of Alice's plan was finalized on the spot, and they promised Alice an update within the week. When the case managers got back to their offices, they informed their individual supervisors of the problems in joint management of Alice's case.

If the school board chair had been present at the program managers meeting the next week, she might have been surprised to hear the complaints about the music department cuts. Everybody believed the school was the most appropriate resource to provide music lessons. Jackson was the schools' representative on the program managers team. He said that there was simply no budget for this item. Another of the program managers wanted to kick this problem up to the superintendent and executive directors meetings.

After a brief discussion, the obvious reality was that the school board was not going to restart music education. The program managers would have to find another solution, and probably a good one, because they had learned that music classes were very popular with the kids at the Big Woods Teen Treatment Center. The staff there considered music classes one of the most effective tools available to them, and they had just submitted a grant to expand the music program considerably. Clearly, more kids with enthusiasm for music were going to pop up in the unified case management teams.

Comment
Collaborating to produce better results for clients can mean more work, not less! Fortunately, by splitting up the jobs among partners, the workload is more manageable. In this case, the collaboration's commitment to help youth took it from an immediate focus on a single youth's needs to systems changes at the top level. Even as the direct services staff did "whatever it takes" to keep Alice sober, they pushed the bigger issue out to the executive level of the collaboration, where program and process changes—and requisite financial needs—could be embedded in the system.

At their next meeting, the program managers put together a work group with two people from their team and three other staff outside the collaboration. This work group was instructed to ask the funders of the music program at the treatment facility for funding for a follow-up program in the schools. Meanwhile, Jackson said he would call on the local musicians union for a volunteer to work with Alice. The program managers flagged this issue so that it would stay on their active agenda until a permanent solution was found.

In later months, Alice's enthusiasm for music got her into more trouble. She and some other recovering teens from the other high schools who had also attended Big Woods began to get together and play music. To the vice-principal, who found them practicing in the school auditorium, it looked like a clear violation of the anti-gang policy. After all, here was an unsupervised group of youthful offenders on school property, he argued, clearly in violation of anti-drug and anti-gang policies forbidding teenagers with criminal records from forming groups and meeting at school.

Comment
At its best, a nimble collaboration becomes an opportunity for leaders to revise policies and create better systems. When all the partner organizations are expected to think through policy issues that come up, the system gets changed for the better. Nimble collaborations encourage mutual institution renewal.

Ly went to Jackson's office in a hurry, and this time Jackson and the other program managers didn't wait to meet. They went to the collaboration executive team and asked for clarification of the policy and a decision on Alice's case. The resulting rewrite of the policy by the school board initiated a new look at how to help groups of recovering kids while preventing unhealthy gang activity.

Chapter Summary

This case study demonstrates effective problem solving by a nimble collaboration aimed at service integration at the point of service delivery. Just a few years earlier the teen, Alice, would have had a series of individual meetings with her parole officer and her social services worker. The meetings themselves could easily have taken weeks to arrange.

But the real systems change was the way in which service delivery staff at the frontlines impacted major school policies. When this collaboration structured itself using the target model, it created a pathway for direct communication to leaders about school policies that didn't help kids.

Collaborations that aim at service integration—whether at the point of access, the point of intake and assessment, or the point of service delivery—need deft decision-making and communications structures. Often, service integration is at the heart of a community's efforts to resolve complex issues. Chapter Five looks at the ways in which many organizations within a single community are collaborating around long-term approaches to deeply embedded cultural problems, such as drug abuse or domestic violence. Such collaborations can be even more complicated than service integration collaborations, because service integration is often just one component of the work that needs to get done to change the entire community.

Chapter Five

Collaborate to Resolve Complex Issues

S ome collaborations are trying to resolve complex issues in their communities using multiple strategies, multiple organizations, and a long-term commitment— perhaps ten years or more. For example:

> In Houston, a group of foundations, public institutions, nonprofits, and community groups are attempting to change the infrastructure for providing children's daycare, including licensing provisions, teaching methodologies, and access for parents.

> Many rural counties and parishes, towns, townships, and cities are coming together to develop regional plans for economic development and tourism. In the West, one such collaboration has created an economic and ecological plan supported by literally every organization in the region that promotes tourism and the environment.

> In New Jersey, the United Way of Essex and West Hudson is creating "councils" composed of the leaders of many collaboratives in the Greater Newark area. The United Way instigated these councils as it saw many duplicative funding requests for collaborations aimed at improving services, products, and communities. By bringing the partners together in a kind of "collaboration of collaborations," the United Way is supporting New Jersey agencies' vision of enhanced services.

This chapter delves into the special nature of nimble collaborations that use multiple strategies and groups to develop communitywide social policies or to intervene in complex issues. While all of the suggestions in this book apply to such collaborations, some particular best practices are emerging:

- Enlist a highly visible spokesperson
- Modify partner agencies' mission statements

- Eliminate meeting overlap
- Retreat and reflect
- Conduct mutual evaluations
- Use a community-driven process to distribute funds

Use These Emerging Best Practices

Many of the existing collaborations devoted to complex issues resolution are new, coming into place only during the last five to eight years. Thus, experience keeping complex, communitywide collaborations going is limited. Here, however, are some of the emerging best practices.

Enlist a highly visible spokesperson

Collaborations working to change the culture of a community often find that an influential public person can make a major difference in changing public perceptions. Such collaborations may choose a celebrity or a well-known community or business leader to keep the issue in the public eye. This champion wields power and public face to keep the issue in the forefront of public decision making. The champion doesn't have to come from Hollywood but does need wide public recognition in the collaboration's own town.

Modify partner agencies' mission statements

Chapter 1 spoke of the collaboration's mission statement as a placeholder, making room for each partner agency's mission statement. But at the large end of the collaboration scale, partner agencies are turning this practice on its head: *They are changing their individual mission statements to reflect the mission of the collaboration.* Such changes show the depth of the partner agencies' commitment to the goal of the collaboration. They also ensure that the work of the collaboration is continued beyond the tenure of the agency representative, and even beyond the membership of the organization in the collaboration, because the agency itself has changed. For example, a variety of organizations in Ramsey County, Minnesota, have decided that violence is a key barrier to their goals. Domestic abuse shelters, teen clubs, and law enforcement agencies have all added a phrase to their individual mission and philosophy statements that emphasizes their commitment to reduce violence as part of their mission.

Eliminate meeting overlap

Collaborations to resolve complex issues don't always start that way. Often they evolve over time. As more collaborations emerge around related issues, agency representatives find themselves showing up at two or three different collaboration meetings weekly, often involving many of the same people. The organizations and their representatives are involved in a complex issues collaboration, even before they realize it. A first step in coming to grips with the realities of multiple collaborations and collaborations of collaborations is to eliminate the intense overlap of meetings that occurs. More productive linkages can help save time and frustration. Here is an example of how one town handled this.

> In a small town in the Midwest, the collaborations around social services integration, elimination of substance abuse, teen crime, and family health were all active and well funded . . . and staffed by the same people from the same small local government and nongovernment organizations. Frequently, the very same people could be seen at successive meetings during the week, all on different topics. These (tired!) collaboration partners decided to save on meeting time. They came up with the following procedures: Every other Monday morning the executives and leaders meet and cover all the issues they need to cover on all the collaborations they're engaged in. On alternate Monday mornings the midlevel administrators and program managers meet for the same reasons.
>
> This procedure has cut many meetings out of the schedules of these overworked partners. For example, the assistant school superintendent estimated savings of eight hours of weekly meeting time!

The people and agencies involved in the example above are all working to change a complex set of social problems that have a negative impact on their individual clients. While they don't recognize it as such, they have embarked on a collaboration of collaborations, aimed at improving the linked risk factors and ultimately changing the culture of their community. The simple step of reducing meeting overlap is a signal of their movement in this direction.

Retreat and reflect

All collaborations need to take time to retreat and reflect on their successes and challenges, and it is especially important that in large collaborations the whole body assemble. Direct service staff can hear from leaders about current challenges, and vice versa. And the sheer numbers of people who show up can make an emotional difference to staff who may be experiencing mission exhaustion.

Conduct mutual evaluations

Most evaluations conducted in a collaboration focus on the changes in the services or products offered to consumers. Some collaborations also evaluate their partnership. But, if the essence of a nimble collaboration is mutual institutional renewal, then the most important evaluation is organization-to-organization. This evaluation answers the question, "How is each agency changing internally to help the whole system?" When collaborating organizations choose this route, they can conduct mutual evaluations, working together to examine each other's organizations.

> In a midsize town out West, the five major partners in a special education collaboration met to evaluate each organization's participation. Good news and bad news about each partner was generated in general discussion. For instance, the good news about the mental health center was its support and respect for special education teachers' needs. The bad news was how often it was not represented at important meetings. When the facilitator called for action steps at the end of the meeting, the action step for the mental health center was to assign a specific individual to attend all the collaboration meetings. The good news for the school district was its ability to alter certain policies to allow children better access to special education. The bad news was its failure to act as a responsive fiscal agent— it often took months for other partners to get reimbursed. The school district's action step was to improve turnaround time for cutting checks.

Use a community-driven process to distribute funds

When collaborations take on complex, communitywide issues, they must pay careful attention to the distribution of resources. Often there's good news for such projects: The collaborations are so successful that they attract money and community resources. The challenge is that partners must figure out how to distribute funds fairly and without evoking destructive competition among partners. A four-step process, described next, maintains the principles of nimble collaboration while establishing a method to distribute funds fairly. These four steps are

1. The community sets priorities
2. Collaboration partners create a budget
3. Agencies make bids
4. Organizations that do the work allocate the funds

1. The community sets priorities

The first step in any funds allocation process for a complex issue collaboration must include the community and consumers as well as staff and leaders from the collaborating agencies. At least one communitywide meeting should be held, usually hosted by a recognized leader: the mayor or county board member or some other elected official. The purpose of this meeting is to get community input for prioritizing tangible results the collaborating programs might accomplish. The core members of the collaboration may use needs assessment data and other data to describe the needs the members see. This list of needs can serve as a "menu" from which community members can prioritize the results they want.

This meeting offers an added advantage: Service providers can inform the community about services already available to the community, so some education and public relations work is done.

2. Collaboration partners create a budget

Next, the collaboration partners work to predict costs for carrying out the community-driven priorities. For instance, citizens list after-school crime reduction as a top priority. The county has $100,000 in new grant money to spend. How much of that money will be spent on this outcome? There's plenty of negotiation during this time as agencies try to determine how much of the new resources to spend on which efforts. These negotiations tend to emphasize results and tangible outcomes. Instead of talking about programming, administrators begin to talk to each other about who is accountable for what result.

3. Agencies make bids

Next, individual agencies show what they already do related to the outcomes the public has prioritized—what the current work costs and where the resources come from. For instance: How much does it cost for a parole agent to track a juvenile offender? How much does it cost for a person to use county and state employment services? How much does the teen pregnancy prevention program cost? This step builds trust among agencies by sharing data and proving the quality of services being provided.

Then the agencies make bids against the new money that is available. Each agency submits a bid that includes which results it expects to achieve, the work it will undertake to achieve those results, and how much the work will cost the agency. For instance, a collaboration decides to reduce after-school adolescent crime. Regional corrections submits a bid for two new full-time juvenile parole officers. The parks department submits a bid for more sports programs after school. The scouting clubs submit a bid for creating four more troops, and the schools submit a bid for after-school learning enrichment activities. These are all activities that might achieve the result of lower after-school crime, and each agency proposes the part of the work it does the best.

Overlapping bids are handled by the agencies themselves, not some removed group that "awards" funds. If two groups want to do after-school sports, they work together to eliminate duplications. If necessary, the collaboration can provide a facilitator to help partners work out their differences. Agencies that once might have competed now submit dovetailed applications or have just one agency submit a bid. Agencies get clear with each other about whether they can offer what the work needs, and they avoid submitting grants that will go unfunded. The result: All funding applications go into a complete, sensible, and affordable package that expresses the priorities of the community.

At its own home office, each agency should be planning budget changes to respond to the community priorities and to work effectively with other organizations in the collaboration.

4. Organizations that do the work allocate the funds

An open bidding process—every member of the collaborative reads all the bids—avoids secretive competitive proposals. Each agency knows how much money is available and what everybody else wants to do, so service gaps and opportunities are spotted by the bidding agencies, not just by a distant funder. This process avoids a possible Catch-22: members of a collaboration using a competitive process to allocate resources.

The elected officials, in the case of public funding, or foundation program officers, for private funding, sign off on the package that's selected, abiding by this principle: Resources—hard cash or in-kind—are *expected* from every partner. And, resources—hard cash or in-kind—are *distributed* to the partners who do the work.

This process engages the whole community—not just the staff of the partner agencies—in enhancing services. When public money is at stake, the process puts the responsibility for spending tax dollars and shared community resources where it belongs: with elected officials and the community they represent. When private foundation money is being allocated, the process avoids the kinds of overlap funders often complain about.

These are just a few examples of the creative ways that large, complex collaborations are sustaining themselves over time. As your collaboration experiments with the three Rs of nimble collaboration—results, relationships, and resilience—it will discover more techniques. The following case study shows how one large collaboration creatively manages the work around a major social issue in the community.

Collaboration mystery revealed

Author and management guru Ken Blanchard teaches: "The kind of thinking that led to past success will not lead to future success."[20] This goes double for the nimble collaboration.

Case study: Baker County, Oregon, tackles drug abuse

Most of the case studies in this book focus on the immediate effect the collaboration has on its customers and users. This case study tells the story of how a group of leaders in a town birthed and nurtured a complex collaboration whose aim—the elimination of drug abuse—can only be achieved over several generations. When reading the case study, look for sidebars that point out ways in which this group addressed results, relationships, and resiliency to stay nimble over the long haul.

---

[20] Ken Blanchard et al., *Empowerment Takes More Than a Minute* (New York: MJF Books, 1996), 2.

In Baker County, Oregon, during the mid-1990s, economic and community development initiatives were successfully implemented by a group of businesspeople who called their work together "Community Partnership I." Since 1996 this group—which includes businesses, economic development bodies, and city and county representatives—has secured resources and planned strategic changes collaboratively. Partnership I was such a success that an important private foundation challenged the group to grow collaborations in social services as well. Thus was born "Community Partnership II" in 1997.

The mission of Community Partnership II is to "make Baker County the premier rural living experience through a strategic plan to eliminate the abuse of alcohol and drugs and resulting harm to our community." The social support organizations include the mental health center, the treatment center, county social services, public health, schools, law enforcement, and the domestic abuse shelter. These agencies are energized by their vision that all of Baker County's children grow up free of harm from the abuse of alcohol and illegal drugs.

Comment
Partnership II engaged many organizations and individual residents in the creation of its vision, and it wrote a mission statement that related directly to the mission of Partnership I. (See pages 20–22 on mission and vision for instructions on how to do this.) By getting input from many different stakeholders and by relating the effort to an existing, successful group, these leaders built in sustainability for their work.

While the benefits of a substance-abuse-free community may seem obvious, this mission was only developed over time. The Baker County Commission on Children and Families convened countless meetings in various parts of the county among many constituencies to discuss the mission. Some of the most rural communities in the county didn't believe a drug problem impacted them, and Partnership II worked hard to uncover those communities' self-interest in the collaboration. Leaders from the better-known Partnership I became visible spokespeople for Partnership II by helping businesses see how the bottom line was impacted by employees with substance-abuse problems.

The collaboration got off to a vigorous start. The local foundation awarded grants to seven projects to collaboratively reduce abuse of alcohol and other drugs. These projects met stringent criteria and each organization committed to a long-range undertaking (five to ten years) to focus on substance abuse.

As the collaboration evolved, senior community leaders assembled at a monthly meeting (called the "Progress Board") to keep track of activities and successes. Senior administrators and program managers met in a separate group to keep a sharp focus on the work of family social support systems, such as welfare and the treatment center. This group came to see itself as the core members of Partnership II.

The core members did a great job of delegating decision making to smaller, task-oriented committees. This delegation system occasionally failed them. Some grantwriting or report-producing responsibilities got confused or lost steam. Partnership II currently holds retreats once or twice a year to revive energy and recommit to the mission of a substance-abuse-free community.

Comment

Partnership II has stayed nimble by keeping smaller groups of the right people doing the right thing. (See the discussion of roles, pages 41–50.) Partners modify members' expectations of one another by clarifying who is accountable for what activity. They don't bring everyone to the table for every issue, but only those members necessary to make the decision. (See the membership ring, page 40, and the discussion of decision making, pages 58–63.)

The results of all this work are impressive. New resources have been uncovered and inefficiencies in using existing resources corrected. For example, professionals worked with local law enforcement to determine the fifteen individuals and families that generated the most substance-abuse-related police calls. As unified case management and collaborative treatment plans worked for those people, other families demanded to be included. By 1999 the partners agreed to handle at least 50 percent of their recovery clients using the unified case management process. They expect it to be 100 percent in the near future.

In 1999 the core partner organizations also met to exchange honest feedback about ways each of the agencies must change to best serve clients. All the time spent in developing relationships paid off as individuals identified clear programmatic deficiencies in each organization. Later in the year they restructured the collaboration to lessen their reliance on the coordinator and strengthen their accountability to one another.

Partnership II's efforts to integrate services were rewarded in 2000. That year the Oregon State Department of Human Services awarded Baker County funding and special assistance to pilot a groundbreaking effort, completely integrating all the services offered by the Department of Human Services in Baker County. Such a massive undertaking taxed the ability of many organizations. Several meetings that year focused on roles and accountabilities of individual organizations to the collaboration. Leadership was an issue as well; with many of the largest social support agencies deeply engaged in service integration, the coordination function for the collaboration got bogged down or lost. The role of the coordinator had to be resurrected and restructured.

The members of Partnership II have dealt with conflicts about roles and accountabilities as openly as possible, bringing systems issues to the table and discussing them. Sometimes decisions have been made easily; at other times there have been difficult days and tension. A consultant has been called in on a regular basis to help.

Comment

Baker County's Partnership II is an excellent example of a complex issue resolution collaboration that employs service integration (the subject of Chapter Four) as one of its strategies.

Most recently Community Partnership II members met to expand their efforts. Certainly, their commitment to eliminate alcohol and drug abuse is not abated; it is simply obvious that collaboration is a great way to help people on a larger scale. Today its mission reads: "Community Partnership II supports Baker County as the premiere rural living experience in the Pacific Northwest by renewing and improving social support and service systems, procuring new resources for those systems, and championing specific tasks."

Partnership II is guided by these points as it moves forward on its mission:

- "All service providers, including private nonprofit entities, are full partners.

- "All partners and team leaders add value with their diverse skill sets, resources and supports.

- "The focus is on the customer rather that on the process most familiar to the service provider.

- "We encourage creativity and innovation for clients, including the use of public-private collaborations, multi-disciplinary teams and part-time contractual workers.

- "Public dollars are leveraged to generate more resources and to improve client outcomes.

- "We support agreements between governments, agencies and non-profits to share financial and human resources, infrastructure and training. Whatever it takes!

- "We respect client confidentiality; it is not a barrier to providing multi-disciplinary solutions. Partnership II release of information permits information sharing among partners for unified case management.

- "We are committed to including the family in [our work and] in community-based solutions.

- "Regular partnership meetings and workgroups manage multi-agency cases, review outcomes, and provide a collaborative forum for system improvements. Individual agencies will be asked to make changes to improve the system.

- "Strong, capable leaders work together to remove barriers.

- "[We hold ourselves accountable] with specific dates and measures for achievement of outcomes by clients and providers."[21]

If you are engaged in a collaboration addressing complex, long-term social issues, then the story of Baker County's Community Partnership II can help you take steps to correct problems, manage conflict effectively, and nimbly make decisions.

Chapter Summary

As a tool, collaboration is uniquely suited to tackling the resolution of a complex issue or to changing a broad social policy. Because such efforts require the long-term commitment of many organizations from all sectors of society, it is important to use best practices in order to stay nimble. Since the early 1980s, when the potential for collaborations began to be explored, much has been learned about the processes that make shorter-term, smaller partnerships effective. The strategies of focusing on results, building relationships, and enhancing resiliency make those partnerships work. Those strategies are also effective in more complex, social-policy-driven collaborations. But these special, multiple-generation partnerships face special challenges, and wise partners learn to nimble-ize their collaboration to be the most responsive to the current environment.

---

[21] The author is grateful to the Baker County Commission on Children and Families for permission to cite the success of Partnership II and to quote from its reports.

Conclusion

The Power of Collaboration

Collaborating has proved to be an important process for joining organizations interdependently to achieve some result that cannot be achieved independently. We no longer need to ask ourselves, "Shall we work together?" We now need to ask, "What is the best time and the best way to work together?" Old assumptions about collaborations are giving way to fresher, more productive methods of partnering. These new methods revolve around three strategies.

A *focus on results* is the strategy that keeps the prize in front of us. Results are statements of specific, measurable outcomes that we can achieve together in a reasonable time frame. Knowing whether partners are cooperating, coordinating, or collaborating helps clarify the contribution each organization is making. As members of nimble collaborations, we don't assume responsibility for these desired results in the vacuum of a meeting room. Rather, we pursue active support for these results from the most powerful leaders in our organizations, and we champion these results in the everyday work at each of our home offices.

Successful partners recognize that collaborating is what's needed to solve the most complex problems, the problems that allow clients to fall through the cracks in the system or that interfere with effective use of resources. No matter what system we are working in—education, health, human services, the arts, community development, or any other system—our organizations need to collaborate to fix that system. And to change the system each of its parts must change. To get the desired results, each organization must modify the way it does business.

So each part of the system must learn from the others. Each organization must reflect on what it is and what it does in relation to other organizations. *Shaping relationships* is the second important strategy for nimble collaboration, because trusting relationships make this reflection safe. In a nimble collaboration, we don't call all the organizations to the meeting table and hope they stay invested. Rather, we name the core partners and clarify the roles of other groups who are important to our work. We understand and work with self-interest. We put our organizations' needs out in the open, and openly discuss the needs of others. Instead of battling over turf issues and hidden agendas, we respect the values and contributions of the agencies who are part of the system. Together, we know, we can make a difference.

So over the last decade, the question has morphed from "Is it a good idea to work together?" to "How can we stay the course to get the results we want?" In a nimble collaboration, we use the strategy of *resilience* to craft a powerful, flexible, sustainable partnership. We use the ten principles of resilience in our everyday work and in the creation of a governance system for the collaboration. We sustain our work over time by documenting our governance system, and by using those documents to influence the most powerful leaders in our communities.

Perhaps as a result of being part of collaborations that have crashed and burned, we have learned that if there's a problem in our services or programs, we just get busy and fix it. We coordinate or cooperate to solve a problem with an obvious solution. We save the arduous process of collaborating for those problems that don't have a simple answer or for building communitywide responses to complex issues.

Today, when we agree to enter into and build a collaboration, we know we're getting ready to make changes inside our own organizations. As we learn about what our constituents need, and what our agencies do, we change ourselves in the context of the whole system.

We've expanded our definition of collaboration: It is a relationship entered into by two or more organizations to achieve a result no one organization can achieve alone, and it is a commitment to the mutual institutional renewal that embeds the results for lasting success.

Just as some of us remember what it was like to work every day with an electric typewriter—not a computer—some of us know what it is like to try to build better communities from within a shell, without access to other organizations in the community. In every county or parish, in every state and province, we are insisting on collaboration as a way out of the shell. This book testifies to the power of working together. Your work in partnership is witness to the potent changes for kids, parents, couples, singles, and seniors—for the community and the systems that shape it—when we agree to undergo the precipitous work of collaboration.

Appendix A

Sample Forms

Program Financial Information 111

Write a Memo of Agreement for Your Collaboration 113

Draft a Formal Governance Agreement 115

An electronic version of Program Financial Information may be downloaded from the publisher's web site. Use the following URL to obtain this form

http://www.wilder.org/pubs/workshts/pubs_worksheets1.html?288ncm

This online form is intended for use in the same way as a photocopy of the form, but it is in a format that allows you to type in your responses and modify the form to fit your collaboration. Please do not download the form unless you or your organization has purchased this workbook.

INSTRUCTIONS: Each partner should fill in the information below in preparation for sharing financial information. The goal of financial disclosure is to improve the service delivery system. (See the section Expose detailed financial information on page 64 for more information.)

1. Submitted by _____

(Name of Organization)

on _____

(Date)

2. This form allows core collaboration members to share financial information regarding existing programming related to the following collaboration outcome:

3. Name of the agency program related to this outcome:

4. Fill out the table below. In column 1, name each program, service, or product
   delivered by the agency that fulfills the collaboration outcome specified in
   question 2 above. In column 2, state the amount spent on that program and
   the source (fee, government contract, and so forth). In column 3, state what
   one unit of service costs. Be sure to define the unit of service in advance of
   the meeting to share financial information.

Programs, Services, and Products	Total Amount Spent and Source of Funds	Cost of Service Unit

INSTRUCTIONS: Ask each partner organization to write a memo of agreement addressed to all the partners in the collaboration. In this memo, consider including

- A list of the partners that your leadership or board believes is participating in the effort.
- A description of the vision and mission that drives the collaboration.
- A description of the outcomes or results that the collaboration wants to achieve, and your board's commitment to getting those results.
- A statement of your organization's self-interest and, if possible, a statement of resources that your organization is prepared to dedicate to the effort.

The sample below can serve as a guide.

A Sample Memo of Agreement

Playspace Collaboration
c/o Family Daycare Center
Pleasantville, USA

Dear Collaboration Partners:

The Community Garden wants to be an active member in the collaborative work to revitalize children's parks and play spaces in Pleasantville. We understand that the other partners are the Family Daycare Center, the University Arboretum, the City of Pleasantville Parks Department, and School District #202.

We are committed to making the joint decisions that will be required if the collaboration is to achieve its desired results. We understand those results include

- New landscaping and equipment in the outdoor play space at the Community Garden, the Daycare Center, the Arboretum, and Washington Elementary School.
- New interior gymnastics equipment for Jefferson Middle School.
- 50 percent increase in the use of play spaces by children under 13 during summer, 2003.

We are contributing our executive director's time to attend meetings, and have authorized her to make decisions as appropriate. We also agree to be the fiscal agent for any grants awarded to the collaboration. We will provide these fiscal services for a fee of 2 percent of the total grant award.

Our self-interests include improving our own playground at the Garden in midtown, and making use of public relations opportunities to promote the Garden as a family activity. We are especially concerned about grooming the goodwill of our volunteers. As a board we have discussed the need to make some changes in order to have the best volunteer system possible. We await information from our executive director about this matter.

We expect to remain engaged in dialogues and to do our share of the work in order to get results. Thank you to all the partners for working with us.

Board Chair
The Community Garden

INSTRUCTIONS: Write a governance agreement for your collaboration. Consider including the key elements of governance systems as explained in this book. You do not have to include all the following elements; simply use the list as a starting point.

- The vision of your collaboration
- The mission of your collaboration
- The intended outcomes of your collaboration
- Your evaluation criteria
- Your work plan
- A complete list of organizations that are core partners in the collaboration
- A list of organizations that are cooperating or coordinating with the collaboration
- A statement of self-interest for each organization
- Role descriptions for each organization as a whole and for individual representatives from each organization
- A job description for the coordinator, if there is one
- A plan to communicate key information to organizations in your collaboration
- A process for decision making in your collaboration
- A process for creating joint budgets and other financial documents relating to your collaboration
- A list of legal documents needed for your collaboration

The sample document on the following page lays out some basic structures in an agreement among three community organizations that provide food to the hungry in a mid-sized town. All the executives of the partner organizations in this collaboration signed the agreement. Notice that this agreement does not include all of the elements listed above, just the ones most important to this particular collaboration at this time.

A SAMPLE FORMAL GOVERNANCE AGREEMENT

Emergency Food Services Collaboration

Mission statement

The agencies listed below agree that the present system of feeding hungry people in our community does not always meet those families' needs, and sometimes wastes precious resources. Therefore:

> We want to feed every hungry person in or near his or her home, provide a safety net for the homeless hungry, and generate more resources to feed families.

Outcomes

We are working in a collaborative effort to accomplish our vision and mission. We will know we are successful when we have the following outcomes.

1. *We report collateral, consistent information to our public by using the same counting system for describing our food services.* Every organization will report to funders and the public with parallel statistics—a system to be designed during our collaborative effort. For instance, we will all agree to count food poundage, numbers of individuals fed, and households served.

2. *We shape a cohesive public identity by using a collaborative system for food donations and collections.* For instance, we will eliminate duplicate collection bins at the same site, and coordinate decisions about collection activities before we begin to work with other agencies.

3. *We work to avoid "holes" in the emergency food provision system by publishing guidelines for agencies, the city, the county, and funders to use (and by meeting together to plan services; see outcome #4 below).* For instance, we will jointly write guidelines for how many soup kitchens, food shelves, or food banks our community needs and other key questions. These guidelines are not meant to "run" individual organizations but to inform leaders of needs and challenges as programs develop.

4. *We work to avoid duplication of services by planning for service changes.* Together we will help shape the business relationships among agencies and providers, give input on policies regarding a new revolving food account program, support agencies' efforts to establish this program, and share our counsel on seeking funds for high-price items such as refrigerator equipment.

Note: This part of the agreement was signed by each of the board chairs of the agencies and the area administrator for the state Health and Human Services Department.

Work plan

In order to achieve our desired outcomes, we will follow this work plan:

Tasks to Do	Criteria for Excellence	Agency Primarily Responsible	Deadline or Schedule
Convene workshop of funders	All five major funders rate the workshop excellent	Agency A	By August 1
etc.	*etc.*	*etc.*	*etc.*

Note: The "work plan" section of this sample shows just enough to give a sense of what the collaboration's work plan looked like.

Roles of member agencies

Agency A agrees to offer meeting space for all regularly scheduled partner meetings at no cost.

Agency B will provide food service for meetings, workshops, and events.

Agency C agrees to provide up to 2 hours per week of clerical work if necessary. The collaboration will reimburse Agency C at the rate of $12.50 per hour to total no more than $100 per month for clerical assistance.

At this time the collaboration has no staff. We have contracted with Smith Associates to provide consultation, technical advice, and limited documentation production. That contract is concluded on December 31, 2003, and (as indicated in the above table) we will decide by November 15, 2003, whether or not to extend the contract.

We plan to create a staff position for marketing and public relations. When that position is funded and filled, one of the collaboration partners will provide office space, one of the partners will provide daily supervision and performance feedback, and the fiscal agent will pay salary. Agencies to fulfill these roles will be selected when the position is advertised.

Finances

The Department of Health and Human Services agrees to act as the collaboration fiscal agent, receiving moneys from grantors and partner agencies, creating appropriate fiscal records and audit trails, and disbursing funds as required. See the work plan for the grantwriting schedule.

Process charter

The agencies taking part in this collaboration agree that:

1. NEW AGENCY MEMBERS will be added when the partners signing this document decide to add them. This decision will be made during regular collaboration meetings. New members can ask to join, or a partner can nominate them to join. New members will be added if a majority of existing partners is in favor. All new members must show basic organization health, including an intact board, the board chair's support for membership in the collaboration, positive financial statements, and statements of mission, outcomes, programs, plans, and client goals.

2. EACH MEMBER sends an agency representative, an individual who represents his or her organization. Each agency representative is expected to keep the home agency apprised of collaboration events, decisions, and discussions. Any agency representative can ask for assistance from the group to get his or her agency to buy into decisions partners are making. At least once a year the board of each agency will review and approve of the actions of the collaboration. Each agency representative is expected to attend all regularly scheduled partner meetings, or to assign a substitute representative with whom he or she is in close contact.

3. WE MAKE DECISIONS at regularly scheduled collaboration meetings by consensus if possible. When we must, we vote with majority ruling. Decisions must be made in the atmosphere of mutual benefit. Specific decisions can be delegated to staff, consultants, task forces, or others, ONLY after we have decided to delegate such a decision during a regularly scheduled collaboration meeting.

4. CONFLICT is a normal part of collaboration, and we seek to find creative resolutions to our conflicts. When consultants are employed, they have the right to intervene and direct our conflict dialogues. If we cannot resolve a conflict we will (1) employ a conflict mediation firm or (2) turn the conflict over to our superiors in our organizations and ask them to resolve the issues.

5. WE WILL REWARD OURSELVES with a midsummer evening barbecue for partners and their key staff and board members. When we achieve outcome #3, we will publish the guidelines with a lot of media publicity!

Appendix B

Resources

The following books, articles, and publications are helpful in thinking through the complex processes of nimble collaboration.

Angelica, Emil. *The Wilder Nonprofit Field Guide to Crafting Effective Mission and Vision Statements.* St. Paul, MN: Amherst H. Wilder Foundation, 2001.

Bennis, Warren. *Why Leaders Can't Lead.* San Francisco: Jossey-Bass, 1989.

Bennis, Warren, and Patricia Ward. *Organizing Genius: The Secrets of Creative Collaboration.* New York: Addison-Wesley, 1997.

Blanchard, Ken et al. *Empowerment Takes More Than a Minute.* New York: MJF Books, 1996.

Block, Peter. *Flawless Consulting.* San Diego: Pfeiffer, 1981.

Brumburgh, Scott et al. "Literature Review and Model Framework of Nonprofit Capacity Building." In *Innovation Network.* Washington, D.C.: Environmental Support Center, 2000.

Cox, Gary. "Model Agreement for Children's Collaboratives in Minnesota." St. Paul, MN: Minnesota Department of Human Services, Jan. 1998.

Flower, Joe. "Collaboration: The New Leadership." *Healthcare Forum Journal,* November/December, 1995.

Guza, Terry et al. *OIS Service Integration Needs Assessment Project, Final Report.* Portland, OR: Oregon Department of Human Services, May 2001.

Hicks, Bone. *Self-Managing Teams.* Los Altos, CA: Crisp Publications, 1999.

Himmelman, Arthur. *Resolving Conflict: Strategies for Local Government.* Washington, D.C.: International City/County Management Association, 1994.

Kagan, Sharon L. *United We Stand: Collaboration for Child Care and Early Education Services*. New York: Teachers College Press, 1991.

La Piana, David. *The Nonprofit Mergers Workbook*. St. Paul, MN: Amherst H. Wilder Foundation, 2000.

Mattessich, Paul, Marta Murray-Close, and Barbara Monsey. *Collaboration: What Makes It Work*. Second Edition. St. Paul, MN: Amherst H. Wilder Foundation, 2001.

Parker-Carlson, Jessica et al. *Points of Access Research Report*. Anoka, MN: Anoka County Children and Family Council, 2001.

Scherer, J., and J. Sherwood. "A Model for Couples: How Two Can Grow Together." *Journal of Small Group Behavior,* Vol. 6 No. 1, February 1975.

Schrage, Michael. *No More Teams: Mastering the Dynamics of Creative Collaboration*. New York: Currency-Doubleday, 1995.

Size, Tom. "Managing Collaborations: The Perspective of a Rural Hospital Cooperative." *Health Care Management Review*. New York: Aspen Publishers, 1994.

Stacey, Ralph. *Managing the Unknowable: Strategic Boundaries Between Order and Chaos in Organizations*. San Francisco: Jossey-Bass, 1992.

Winer, Michael, and Karen Ray. *Collaboration Handbook: Creating, Sustaining, and Enjoying the Journey*. St. Paul, MN: Amherst H. Wilder Foundation, 1994.

MANAGEMENT & PLANNING

Consulting with Nonprofits: A Practitioner's Guide

by Carol A. Lukas

A step-by-step, comprehensive guide for consultants. Addresses the art of consulting, how to run your business, and much more. Also includes tips and anecdotes from thirty skilled consultants.

240 pages, softcover   *Item # AWF-98-CWN*

The Wilder Nonprofit Field Guide to
Crafting Effective Mission and Vision Statements

by Emil Angelica

Guides you through two six-step processes that result in a mission statement, vision statement, or both. Shows how a clarified mission and vision lead to more effective leadership, decisions, fundraising, and management. Includes tips on using the process alone or with an in-depth strategic planning process, sample mission and vision statements, step-by-step instructions, and worksheets.

88 pages, softcover   *Item # AWF-01-FMV*

The Wilder Nonprofit Field Guide to
Developing Effective Teams

by Beth Gilbertsen and Vijit Ramchandani

Helps you understand, start, and maintain a team. Provides tools and techniques for writing a mission statement, setting goals, conducting effective meetings, creating ground rules to manage team dynamics, making decisions in teams, creating project plans, and developing team spirit.

80 pages, softcover   *Item # AWF-99-FGD*

The Five Life Stages of Nonprofit Organizations
Where You Are, Where You're Going, and What to Expect
When You Get There

by Judith Sharken Simon with J. Terence Donovan

Understand your organization's current stage of development and prepare it to move ahead to the future. Shows you what's "normal" for each development stage which helps you plan for transitions, stay on track, and avoid unnecessary struggles. This unique guide also includes *The Wilder Nonprofit Life Stage*

Assessment. The *Assessment* allows you to plot and understand your organization's "home stage" and gauge your progress in seven arenas of organization development—governance, staff leadership, finance, administrative systems, staffing, products and services, and marketing.

128 pages, softcover   *Item # AWF-01-FLS*

The Lobbying and Advocacy Handbook for Nonprofit Organizations
Shaping Public Policy at the State and Local Level

by Marcia Avner

The Lobbying and Advocacy Handbook is a planning guide and resource for nonprofit organizations that want to influence issues that matter to them. This book will help you decide whether to lobby and then put plans in place to make it work.

240 pages, softcover   *Item # AWF-02-LAH*

The Nonprofit Mergers Workbook
The Leader's Guide to Considering, Negotiating, and
Executing a Merger

by David La Piana

A merger can be a daunting and complex process. Save yourself time, money, and untold frustration with this highly practical guide that makes the process manageable and controllable. This unique guide includes case studies, decision trees, twenty-two worksheets, checklists, tips, milestones, and many examples. You'll find complete step-by-step guidance from seeking partners to writing the merger agreement, dealing with typical roadblocks, implementing the merger, and more.

240 pages, softcover   *Item # AWF-00-NMW*

Resolving Conflict in Nonprofit Organizations:
The Leader's Guide to Finding Constructive Solutions

by Marion Peters Angelica

Helps you identify conflict, decide whether to intervene, uncover and deal with the true issues, and design and conduct a conflict resolution process. Includes exercises to learn and practice conflict resolution skills, guidance on handling unique conflicts such as harassment and discrimination, and when (and where) to seek outside help with litigation, arbitration, and mediation.

192 pages, softcover   *Item # AWF-99-RCN*

Strategic Planning Workbook for Nonprofit Organizations, Revised and Updated

by Bryan Barry

Chart a wise course for your nonprofit's future. This time-tested workbook gives you practical step-by-step guidance, real-life examples, one nonprofit's complete strategic plan, and easy-to-use worksheets.

144 pages, softcover　　　　*Item # AWF-97-SPW*

MARKETING & FUNDRAISING

The Wilder Nonprofit Field Guide to Conducting Successful Focus Groups

by Judith Sharken Simon

Shows how to collect valuable information without a lot of money or special expertise. Using this proven technique, you'll get essential opinions and feedback to help you check out your assumptions, do better strategic planning, improve services or products, build goodwill, and more.

80 pages, softcover　　　　*Item # AWF-99-FGC*

Coping with Cutbacks:
The Nonprofit Guide to Success When Times Are Tight

by Emil Angelica and Vincent Hyman

Shows you practical ways to involve business, government, and other nonprofits to solve problems together. Also includes 185 cutback strategies you can put to use right away.

128 pages, softcover　　　　*Item # AWF-97-CWC*

The Wilder Nonprofit Field Guide to Fundraising on the Internet

by Gary M. Grobman, Gary B. Grant, and Steve Roller

Your quick road map to using the Internet for fundraising. Shows you how to attract new donors, troll for grants, get listed on sites that assist donors, and learn more about the art of fundraising. Includes detailed reviews of 77 web sites useful to fundraisers, including foundations, charities, prospect research sites, and sites that assist donors.

64 pages, softcover　　　　*Item # AWF-99-FGF*

Marketing Workbook for Nonprofit Organizations Volume I:
Develop the Plan, 2nd Edition

by Gary J. Stern

Don't just wish for results—get them! Here's how to create a straightforward, usable marketing plan. Includes the six P's of Marketing, how to use them effectively, a sample marketing plan, and detachable worksheets.

208 pages, softcover　　　　*Item # AWF-01-MW1*

Marketing Workbook for Nonprofit Organizations Volume II:
Mobilize People for Marketing Success

by Gary J. Stern

Put together a successful promotional campaign based on the most persuasive tool of all: personal contact. Learn how to mobilize your entire organization, its staff, volunteers, and supporters in a focused, one-to-one marketing campaign. Comes with *Pocket Guide for Marketing Representatives*. In it, your marketing representatives can record key campaign messages and find motivational reminders.

192 pages, softcover　　　　*Item # AWF-97-MW2*

Venture Forth! The Essential Guide to Starting a Moneymaking Business in Your Nonprofit Organization

by Rolfe Larson

The most complete guide on nonprofit business development. Building on the experience of dozens of organizations, this handbook gives you a time-tested approach for finding, testing, and launching a successful nonprofit business venture.

272 pages, softcover　　　　*AWF-02-VFB*

COLLABORATION & COMMUNITY BUILDING

Collaboration Handbook:
Creating, Sustaining, and Enjoying the Journey

by Michael Winer and Karen Ray

Shows you how to get a collaboration going, set goals, determine everyone's roles, create an action plan, and evaluate the results. Includes a case study of one collaboration from start to finish, helpful tips on how to avoid pitfalls, and worksheets to keep everyone on track.

192 pages, softcover　　　　*Item # AWF-94-CHC*

Visit us online at www.wilder.org

Collaboration: What Makes It Work, 2nd Edition

by Paul Mattessich, PhD, Marta Murray-Close, BA,
and Barbara Monsey, MPH

An in-depth review of current collaboration research. Major findings are summarized, critical conclusions are drawn, and twenty key factors influencing successful collaborations are identified. Includes The Wilder Collaboration Factors Inventory, which groups can use to assess their collaboration.

104 pages, softcover   Item # AWF-01-CWW

Community Building: What Makes It Work

by Wilder Research Center

Reveals twenty-eight keys to help you build community more effectively. Includes detailed descriptions of each factor, case examples of how they play out, and practical questions to assess your work.

112 pages, softcover   Item # AWF-97-CBW

Community Economic Development Handbook

by Mihailo Temali

The most comprehensive book available on revitalizing distressed communities.

275 page, softcover   *(available Fall 2002)*

The Nimble Collaboration
Fine-Tuning Your Collaboration for Lasting Success

by Karen Ray

Shows you ways to make your existing collaboration more responsive, flexible, and productive. Provides three key strategies to help your collaboration respond quickly to changing environments and participants.

136 pages, softcover   Item# AWF-02-NCM

VIOLENCE PREVENTION & INTERVENTION

The Little Book of Peace

Designed and illustrated by Kelly O. Finnerty

A pocket-size guide to help people think about violence and talk about it with their families and friends. You may download a free copy of *The Little Book of Peace* from our web site at www.wilder.org.

24 pages (minimum order 10 copies)   Item #AWF-97-LBP
Also available in Spanish and Hmong language editions.

Journey Beyond Abuse: A Step-by-Step Guide to Facilitating Women's Domestic Abuse Groups

by Kay-Laurel Fischer, MA, LP, and Michael F. McGrane, LICSW

Create a program where women increase their understanding of the dynamics of abuse, feel less alone and isolated, and have a greater awareness of channels to safety. This book includes twenty-one group activities that you can combine to create groups of differing length and focus.

208 pages, softcover   Item # AWF-97-JBA

Moving Beyond Abuse: Stories and Questions for Women Who Have Lived with Abuse

(Companion guided journal to Journey Beyond Abuse)

A series of stories and questions that can be used in coordination with the sessions provided in the facilitator's guide or with the guidance of a counselor in other forms of support.

88 pages, softcover   Item # AWF-97-MBA

Foundations for Violence-Free Living: A Step-by-Step Guide to Facilitating Men's Domestic Abuse Groups

by David J. Mathews, MA, LICSW

A complete guide to facilitating a men's domestic abuse program. Includes twenty-nine activities, detailed guidelines for presenting each activity, and a discussion of psychological issues that may arise out of each activity.

240 pages, softcover   Item # AWF-95-FVL

On the Level

(Participant's workbook to Foundations for Violence-Free Living)

Contains forty-nine worksheets including midterm and final evaluations. Men can record their insights and progress.

160 pages, softcover   Item # AWF-95-OTL

What Works in Preventing Rural Violence

by Wilder Research Center

An in-depth review of eighty-eight effective strategies you can use to prevent and intervene in violent behaviors, improve services for victims, and reduce repeat offenses. This report also includes a Community Report Card with step-by-step directions on how you can collect, record, and use information about violence in your community.

94 pages, softcover   Item # AWF-95-PRV

Ordering Information

Order by phone, fax, or online

Call toll-free: **1-800-274-6024**
Internationally: 651-659-6024

Fax: 651-642-2061

E-mail: books@wilder.org
Online: www.wilder.org

Mail: Amherst H. Wilder Foundation
Publishing Center
919 Lafond Avenue
St. Paul, MN 55104

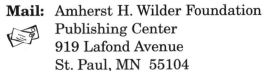

Our NO-RISK guarantee

If you aren't completely satisified with any book for any reason, simply send it back within 30 days for a full refund.

Shipping & handling charges

(to each delivery address)	Ground Service 7-10 business days	Priority Mail * 2-3 business days	Next Day Air * Next day by 5:00 p.m.
If order totals:	*Add:*	*Add:*	*Add:*
Up to $30.00	$4.00	$6.00	$35.00
$30.01 - 60.00	$5.00	$7.00	$40.00
$60.01 - 150.00	$6.00	$8.00	$45.00
$150.01 - 500.00	$8.00	$10.00	$50.00
Over $500.00	3% of order	Call for rate	Call for rate

* Next Day Air orders called or faxed in by 2:00 p.m. EST M-F will be shipped the same day. **All Next Day orders must be prepaid.**

** For priority orders to Canada, please allow 4-7 days for delivery (to clear customs)

Pricing and discounts

For current prices and discounts, please visit our web site at www.wilder.org or call 1-800-274-6024.

Quality assurance

We strive to make sure that all the books we publish are helpful and easy-to-use. Our major workbooks are tested and critiqued by 30-60 experts in the field before being published. Their comments help shape the final book and—we trust—make it more useful to you.

Visit us online

You'll find information about the Wilder Foundation and more details on our books such as table of contents, pricing, discounts, endorsements, and more at www.wilder.org.

Do you have a book idea?

Wilder Publishing Center seeks manuscripts and proposals for books in the fields of non-profit management and community development. To get a copy of our author guidelines, please call us at 1-800-274-6024. You can also download them from our web site at www.wilder.org.